Gender and the Sectional Conflict

Gender

The Steven and
Janice Brose Lectures
in the Civil War Era

WILLIAM A. BLAIR,

EDITOR

and the Sectional Conflict

Nina Silber

THE UNIVERSITY OF NORTH CAROLINA PRESS

Chapel Hill

Designed by Jacquline Johnson
Set in Adobe Caslon
by Keystone Typesetting, Inc.

The paper in this book meets the guidelines for permanence
and durability of the Committee on Production Guidelines
for Book Longevity of the Council on Library Resources.

The University of North Carolina Press has been a member
of the Green Press Initiative since 1993.

Library of Congress Cataloging-in-Publication Data
Silber, Nina.
Gender and the sectional conflict / Nina Silber.
p. cm. — (The Steven and Janice Brose lectures in the
Civil War era)
Includes bibliographical references and index.
ISBN 978-0-8078-3244-8 (cloth: alk. paper)
1. Sex role—United States—History—19th century.
2. United States—History—Civil War, 1861–1865—
Social aspects. 3. United States—History—Civil War,
1861–1965—Women. 4. United States—History—Civil
War, 1861–1865—Causes. 5. Women—United States—
Attitudes—History—19th century. 6. Men—United
States—Attitudes—History—19th century. 7. Patriotism—
United States—History—19th century. 8. United States
Social conditions—19th century. 9. Confederate States of
America—Social conditions. I. Title.
HQ1075.5U68S565 2009
973.7082—dc22
2008017176

cloth 12 11 10 09 08 5 4 3 2 1

To my father,

IRVIN SILBER,

who taught me

the power of history

Contents

Illustrations

Preface

In November 2006 I responded to a very generous request from the Richards Civil War Era Center at Penn State to deliver three lectures as part of the Steven and Janice Brose Distinguished Lecture Series in the Civil War Era. The lectures provided me with an exciting opportunity to take a new spin on an old problem; well, perhaps not an "old" problem by most accounts, but "old" with respect to the research I had been pursuing for a number of years. More specifically, I used the prospect of these lectures as a moment to think about gender and the Civil War from a comparative perspective: to scrutinize different ideas, and practices, regarding manhood and womanhood in the North and South, and among white and black Americans. I also saw this as a chance to take stock of the very rich and, by now, extensive output of scholarship that has been generated in the last fifteen years or so on gender and the sectional conflict, including dozens of books examining white women on both sides of the war, enslaved women and the struggle for emancipation, southern white women and postwar memorial efforts, the wives of Civil War–era presidents and military officers, and women who made unusual wartime contributions as spies, orators, and writers. Now, prodded by the Penn State invitation, I planned to survey this new scholarship, draw on my own research about the Civil War experiences and attitudes of northern women, and place my own findings alongside the considerable literature on Confederate womanhood. I imagined I would find obstacles, both practical and ideological, regarding women's contributions, but that I would also find women, no doubt in distinctive ways, challenging and sometimes overcoming many of those barriers. Aware of recent trends in the scholarship on Confederate women, I may have thought that my

comparative argument would demonstrate how much more northern women were able to do for the Union war effort than southern
women did for the Confederacy and that the success of the Union
military effort hinged, to a considerable extent, on its women.[1]

No doubt northern women did represent a critical asset in the
Union victory. And while I do not ignore the problems of victory
and defeat, my work here is not primarily focused on the "why did
the Confederacy lose and the Union win" debate. That, to put it
mildly, is a scholarly minefield from which few emerge unscathed.
Nor does it seem useful to hone in on the single, or principal, factor
that might explain the South's loss, as it seems more likely that a
broad range of contingent issues—encompassing the military, political, economic, as well as domestic, spheres—shaped the Civil
War's outcome. Steering clear of this intellectual battleground, I
chose instead to pursue a different problem, one initially broached by
LeeAnn Whites in a 1992 essay in which she argued for looking at
the Civil War as a "crisis in gender relations." Looking at "gender
relations," of course, would allow me to broaden my inquiry to
include men as well as women. It would also force me to reckon
with the broader ideological constructions made by northerners and
southerners when they thought about masculinity and femininity.
And, following Whites's lead, I also wanted to look at the "crisis,"
to try to understand something about the sectional battles—pitting
North against South—that seemed to revolve around gender.[2]

Indeed, as Whites observed, the evidence for a crisis seemed extensive: before the war had even started, abolitionist women had at-
tacked the "sinful" domestic life of the slaveholding South; southern white men fretted about the threat that "black Republicanism"
posed to their women; and black men had begun to challenge northern and southern white men's exclusive claim to "manhood." In
making her argument, Whites echoed a long line of scholarship
when she illuminated the way war, not just the Civil War, can
prompt a gender crisis by compelling women to challenge traditional
notions of womanhood as they respond to the new demands im-
posed on them by war. In different times and in different places,

women in war have taken on new roles as nurses, fund-raisers, partisans, and even soldiers, transgressions that have been permitted because they can be cloaked, temporarily, in the guise of patriotism. Thus a young, unmarried woman—in the nineteenth-century South, or in nineteenth-century Britain, or perhaps in twentieth-century France—who leaves her paternal home and puts herself amidst strangers and violence and disease can be commended for the sacrifice she has made for her "cause." War inevitably brings challenges to men as well: they must make sense of war by bringing it into line with their ideas about manhood and masculine obligation. Even more, as in the case of the Confederate South, sometimes they must reconcile their understanding of manhood with the shame of military defeat.[3]

But Whites also touched on something else—not just the way war can inevitably disrupt standard gender relations in any society, but also the way the Civil War, more specifically, took on a distinctive gender framework that reflected historically specific circumstances, most notably the consolidation of racial slavery in the South and the emergence of an idealized and separate domestic sphere in the North. This I saw as the starting point for my lectures: to consider the distinctive gender ideologies of the two sections and understand how those shaped the very different ways in which southerners and northerners thought about the war, how they fought and participated in the war, and ultimately how they remembered the war. My goal was not to argue that differences in gender "caused" the Civil War but rather to see how gender was integral to northerners' and southerners' differing conceptions of why they fought and what the war was about. Most notably, I was intrigued by two concepts that I explored in my first lecture: that both Unionists and Confederates frequently gave women a central place in the way they portrayed wartime objectives, often as a way to lend an immediate and emotional appeal to abstract, political causes; but also that Unionists and Confederates spoke about gender considerations in very different ways when they talked about their respective "causes."

For this first lecture, then, I hoped to make sense of the different ways northerners and southerners thought about "political obligation" in a time of war. To some extent, both northerners and southerners seemed to conform to a standard rhetorical practice when they closely identified the cause for which they were fighting with the women whom they loved. Union and Confederate propaganda gave considerable play to women as defining figures in the struggle, suggesting that women captured the essence of what men laid down their lives for. But while women, homes, and families could be found in the rhetoric of northerners and southerners—not to mention men at war throughout the ages—there were also noteworthy differences across the sectional divide. Most important, Unionists tended to differentiate between the family's "present" welfare and "future" happiness, pledging themselves to fight more for the latter than the former. Even more dramatically, some Unionists pointedly separated their commitment to home from their obligation to the nation and explicitly prioritized the second over the first. In contrast, Confederates blended the causes of home and country and implied that while the nation may have been a cause worth fighting for, it meant nothing in the absence of homes and families.

I had observed this distinction while researching my recent book on Union women and the Civil War, but the Brose lectures, and this current book, allowed me a chance to consider the reasons for the distinction, as well as the implications this distinction had for southern and northern women. Along these lines, I have argued that the different ways in which Unionists and Confederates articulated their causes were not merely rhetorical gestures, nor were they simply reflections of the distinct geographic imperatives encountered by northerners and southerners in the conflict. Rather, they speak to one of the foremost problems that Civil War historians have pondered: the underlying roots of the sectional divide. Again, as I've suggested, I have not argued that gender caused the divide. Like most historians today, I would place myself firmly with those who argue that slavery—in terms of its presence in the southern states and its absence in the northern states—constituted the fundamental divide that caused the conflict. But I would also argue that the division over slavery was not simply a political one, exacerbated by expansion into the western states and the conflict surrounding the admission of those states into the union. The division, I believe, was also reflected in the different socioeconomic orders of the two societies and in the different ideologies by which the residents of those two sections came to understand their roles and identities. And here, I think, is where gender distinctions become so important: they became critical parts of the ideological frameworks adhered to by northerners and southerners. Thus, the increasingly industrialized and market-oriented economy of the northern states ultimately helped to foster an ideology that encouraged men to equate manhood with bread-winning responsibilities outside the home, while women associated womanhood with the moral imperatives of the domestic sphere. On the other hand, the slave-based plantation economy of the South created a more intensely patriarchal orientation among white men who exercised authority over male and female (and black and white) household dependents. Ultimately, I believe much of the language that LeeAnn Whites initially discussed in her essay, language that suggested a wartime "crisis in gender," reflected these distinct ideological orientations. Stated another way, northerners really did believe there were certain ways to be "men" and "women" and that southerners had a pretty poor grasp on what they were. Southerners, for their part, usually thought the same about Yankees.[4]

These distinctive ideologies were, in turn, reflected in the different ways Unionists and Confederates incorporated ideas about home and family into their respective "causes." The Confederate melding of home and country reflected the more intensely patriarchal orientation of the antebellum South; the Unionist prioritizing of nation over home spoke to the extent to which the domestic sphere had been separated from, and made subordinate to, the male breadwinning sphere in the antebellum northern economy. It was also a reflection of the way the nation-state had been, and would become even more so in the course of the war, a more tangible entity in the lives of northern men and women: the purveyor of public education, provider of public assistance, and eventually the guardian of a multimillion-dollar pension fund for Union soldiers and their families. Moreover, as I discuss in Chapter 1, the different ways Unionists and Confederates articulated their military obligations had further repercussions when it came to challenging, or maintaining, traditional ideas about gender, and the actual experiences of women, in the North and the South. Confederates, for their part, idealized Confederate womanhood while they also remained committed to very traditional notions of male protection and female submission, while Unionists ultimately were less bound to traditional expectations regarding women's wartime contributions and even came to expect new degrees of political expression from those in the female sphere. This, ultimately, had important effects on the way men, and women, in the North believed that Union women should express their patriotism.

This topic—female patriotism—comprised the second lecture and what is now the second chapter of this book. Suspecting that being patriotic might have meant different things for Union and Confederate women, I hoped to give further consideration to the problem of female patriotism in the two regions. In particular, I examined how northern and southern women reckoned with traditional notions that denied women the ability to express an autonomous form of patriotism. However, I also wanted to make sense out of something I had encountered in my earlier research but to which I felt I hadn't given adequate attention: why were northern women so intensely berated, more than I think southern women were, for their lack of patriotism during the Civil War? In taking on this topic, I was struck, at first, by a number of similarities: the vastly similar aid societies and relief organizations that women formed in both sections; the comparable types of ceremonies and flag-making rituals that women engaged in; and the nearly identical expressions, at least on the part of elite women, that they were part of a unified female effort that cut across class lines. But I was also struck by the way, midway into the war, northern women seemed to be singled out for their dissipating patriotism and how they were, in almost every case, unfavorably compared with the supposedly more fervent and dedicated female secessionists of the South. I believe a number of factors help explain the attack on northern women's patriotism and, in Chapter 2, I consider such factors as class anxieties, Republican fears of growing Democratic influence, and women's more forthright expressions of their antiwar sentiments. But, in the end, I believe that one of the main reasons northern women were perceived as disloyal, and were repeatedly found wanting in comparison to southern women, was because the Union cause demanded from northern women a kind of patriotic commitment that proved difficult for northern observers to evaluate. In other words, when northerners looked at their womenfolk, they believed that because many women were not enduring hardship at home or personally berating the enemy, they were not being patriotic. Southern women, in contrast, were enduring great hardship and deprivation and had become notorious for their words and acts of defiance toward Union soldiers, all of which made them seem intensely patriotic.

In the end, the attack on northern women's patriotism generated a response, from both men and women, that placed a new premium on women's political autonomy and independent expressions of allegiance. On the one hand, Unionists looked to the South and were no longer prepared to excuse southern women's treasonous actions as nonpolitical manifestations of female loyalty. They were not just women who followed their men, but women who held erroneous political views and acted irresponsibly; as such, they would have to be held accountable. On the other hand, Unionists looked to the North and, to some extent, believed that northern women must also take responsibility for their own political views and actions, and that they must ground their patriotism not simply in traditional womanly obedience but in firm ideological principles.

Still, whatever stigma may have attached itself to Confederate women's treason and disloyalty during the war seemed to be forgiven when Americans looked back upon the war from the vantage point of the late nineteenth century. For my last lecture, and final chapter, I look at the memory of the war, specifically as it related to commemoration by, and about, women. Personally, this lecture gave me a way to come back to some of my earliest research and use it, in a way, to close the circle on gender and the Civil War. It allowed me, too, to look at the tremendous outpouring of literature that has been produced in recent years on Civil War memory. As I argued in the book I published in 1993, *The Romance of Reunion: Northerners and the South, 1865–1900*, Civil War memory was shaped, to a great extent, by ideas about gender, especially in the way northerners adopted a view of the South that highlighted its feminine and domestic virtues and even singled out southern white women as the objects of postwar reconciliation. What I hoped to come back to in my third lecture was the "why" question: why had southern women come to figure so much more prominently, both as leaders of the memorial work and as the objects of commemoration, than northern women? Chapter 3 considers a number of reasons for the memory discrepancies, including the way southern women stepped in when the federal government buried Union soldiers but not Confederates and the interest southern white men had in giving a seemingly neutral face—through women's efforts—to the commemoration of the Confederacy during the Union army's postwar occupation of the South.[5]

In trying to understand the power of southern womanhood on Civil War memories, I also give particular emphasis to the way the Lost Cause movement exploited the traditional Confederate rallying cry to fight for home. Thus it made sense that—as had been true during the war itself—southern white women became central objects of Lost Cause worship. But now I also saw how that worship represented both an extension of Confederate tradition and a fundamental obscuring of the difference between the slave-based plantation "home" and the idealized domestic sphere of the Victorian era. This argument, I believe, clarifies and strengthens the conclusions of my earlier book. It was never my intention to claim that when northerners thought about the South in the years after the war that they replaced their thoughts about race with ideas about gender. As David Blight has demonstrated, questions about race remained crucial and fundamental in the postwar settlements and in sectional reconciliation, especially in the collaboration between northerners and southerners in denying civil and human rights to African Americans. However, as Blight's work has shown, Americans practiced a policy of forgetfulness when it came to race, erasing memories of slavery and emancipation when they thought about the war and focusing instead on union and mutual appreciation. I believe gender played a crucial part in that forgetfulness because it allowed northerners and southerners an especially powerful point of unity—on issues of home and family—issues that had now been completely stripped of their links to racial slavery and the broader racial politics and culture of the prewar and postwar South.[6]

Throughout the work, I have drawn comparisons not only between Union and Confederate but also between whites in both sections and African Americans, both slave and free. That comparison has illuminated a very different tradition among black Americans of linking national cause and gender, of female political autonomy, of remembering the war, and of women's participation in Civil War commemoration. It has also illuminated the extent to which white southerners, when they articulated their obligation to fight for "home" and "family" or when they stepped out in public to remember the Confederate cause, never operated in a racial void but always acted with a clear awareness of the South's racial hierarchy. Still, far more remains to be said about the way gender shaped the African American experience in the Civil War, especially on some of the questions I touch on in this book like patriotism, military obligation, and memory. What I offer here are only very initial and tentative starting points.

Last, I must say something about terms and definitions. Throughout this book, I generally use "northern" and "Unionist" interchangeably, as well as "Confederate" and "southern." This might be a valiant effort to vary my vocabulary, but it does, of course, introduce some misleading simplifications. Across the twenty-three states that did not secede from the Union there was never unified or consistent support for the Union war effort. Indeed, in some regions, especially in southern parts of Ohio, Illinois, and Indiana, as well as in the border states of Missouri, Maryland, Delaware, and Kentucky, there were strong sympathies for the Confederacy. Likewise, across the eleven states that did secede, strong pockets of Unionism could be found. As scholars have begun to suggest, the midsection of the United States in 1861, which crossed over the Mason-Dixon line, seems to have constituted a vast "border region" where there were similar ways of life, like-minded attitudes about race, and strong community, and even family, divisions between Unionists and Confederates. My objective has hardly been to deny this complexity, but my emphasis has been on certain fundamental distinctions, both geographic and ideological, that I believe played a central role in the coming and fighting of the war. In this regard, I am primarily interested in the differences between those who resided in states where slavery had no foothold (what I refer to here as "northern" states) and those who lived where slavery occupied a fundamental place in the social and economic structure ("southern" states). Even more, I am mainly interested in northerners who did as most northerners did and pledged themselves to the Union and in southerners who followed the lead of most of their fellow southerners and pledged themselves to the Confederacy. I do, at certain moments, pay attention to women in the North who expressed anti-Union sentiments. But, for the most part, we must look to future studies to learn more about the war and gender relations among southern Unionists or among border state residents.[7]

I AM GRATEFUL TO many people who contributed to the initial lectures and the final manuscript. I thank Professor William Blair, who directs the Richards Civil War Center at Penn State, for initially extending the invitation to deliver the Brose lectures and for his helpful feedback while I worked on the lectures and when I came to Penn State. Other members of the Penn State faculty also helped me sharpen and strengthen the material I presented. I am especially grateful to Mark Neely, who pressed me on certain points regarding the denunciation of northern women's patriotism and made me think again about John Rogers and his sculpture. I extend my gratitude, too, to Steven and Janice Brose, who have demonstrated a deep and abiding interest in Civil War history, not only in their funding of these lectures, but also by their active participation in the discussions generated by these talks. At my own institution, Boston University, I again benefited from the insight and advice of students and colleagues who read these lectures at various stages. Jack Matthews gave generously of his time, and urged a sharper focus on ideological difference. His suggestions for jokes (in the original lectures but, sadly, omitted from the final manuscript) were also witty and funny and deeply appreciated. The graduate students in my Civil War seminar also patiently endured my discussions of gender and Civil War memory (and read the relevant lecture material) and helped me clarify the points I wished to make. My husband, Louis Hutchins, cast his usual critical eye on my writing, suggested numerous ways to sharpen and tighten the material, and continues to enjoy my love and profound respect.

Gender and the "Cause" in the U.S. Civil War, Union and Confederate

CERTAINLY ONE OF THE most enduring questions asked about war is, "What makes men fight?" Some have also wondered, with perhaps equal persistence, "What makes women send men off to fight?" In the summer of 1914, the German artist Kathe Kollwitz asked a question that could easily have been asked of American women during the Civil War, and of women, and perhaps even of men, today: "Where," Kollwitz queried as German soldiers mobilized for battle, "do all the women who have watched so carefully over the lives of their beloved ones get the heroism to send them to face the canon?" Although the horrors of warfare persist, sadly, to the present day, affecting men as well as women, there have also been some historically specific, and gender-specific, demands placed on the female sex. As Kollwitz wondered, and as Civil War historians might well ponder, Why would women make such enormous sacrifices for a struggle that asked them to do precisely the opposite of what women had always been expected to do: not to nurture their loved ones, but to send them off to die?[1]

Kollwitz's question raises many of the problems at stake when we begin to think about women, war, and the sense of obligation that both men and women feel to serve and sacrifice for their country, not Germany in this case, not during World War I, but northerners and southerners during the U.S. Civil War. Do men go off to war because it is their obligation to protect their women and their families? Or do they fight for a cause that is more abstract and more ideological? Do women sacrifice their husbands because it is one of their wifely obligations to do so, to subordinate themselves to men's demands? Or do women sacrifice their loved ones—send them, in Kollwitz's phrase, "to face the canon"—because they, too, feel allegiance to an abstract and ideological cause? To what extent, in other words, do women feel an obligation to the nation-state, even a nation-state that has done little, if anything, to encourage those women to feel obligated?

Some years ago, the historian James McPherson, building on a recent upsurge in scholarship on soldiers' experiences and motivations, argued that Civil War soldiers, unlike their twentieth-century counterparts, fought with a firm belief in ideological principles. Many scholars contended that World War II troops, most of whom were draftees, fought to prove their courage to friends and comrades, or to demonstrate a sense of masculinity that would win approval from women and society. Civil War soldiers on both sides of the conflict, argued McPherson, most of whom were volunteers, were intensely aware of the issues of government, and many saw their fight as one directly related to the survival of a political state whose beliefs and principles they supported. "If I die for the cause of the Unity entire of this government," wrote one New York man to his widowed mother, "that is the way a man should die." Surveying a broad spectrum of Civil War soldiers, McPherson found similar sentiments echoed in the declarations of numerous enlisted men, as well as officers, on both sides of the sectional divide.[2]

Not that any historian, or anyone who has read anything of Civil War soldiers' letters, would deny the importance of courage and duty and manhood in the soldiers' matrix of motivations. McPherson agrees that these were important factors, but he argues that they did not constitute the essence of what Civil War soldiers fought for. Yet, as a number of contemporary political theorists suggest, we can approach this question another way: not as an either/or proposition, political or personal obligation, but as a melding of the two, in which personal commitments might become a stand-in for politics. Their arguments prompt us to consider the extent to which Civil War soldiers may have spoken of their private responsibilities to home and family as a way to show their investment in a nation-state, a state that, in turn, protected their homes and made possible their private pursuit of happiness. Political theorists have argued that because the liberal state is founded on the basis of a social contract formed among free and independent individuals, compelling those individuals to die on behalf of that state would challenge the very individualism and freedom the liberal state seeks to protect. Consequently, as one historian has suggested, the liberal state "will attempt to exploit private obligations in order to convince its citizens to serve its defense."[3]

Chief among those private obligations has been the protection and preservation of homes, families, and women. Surely it would not be a startling revelation to anyone to argue that the need to serve one's country has often been construed as a duty to fight for women. In countless wars, over the course of human history, men have been pledging themselves to protect their homes and their families against enemy transgressors. What seems to be of particular significance, though, is how—in the history of the modern liberal state—fighting for women has figured prominently as a way to *channel* political and ideological beliefs, and that state officials, along with official and unofficial propagandists, have actively helped to create that sense of private obligation. If American men (or, at least in the nineteenth century, white men) truly were free citizens of a republic, then it follows that they should not be compelled to fight for an arbitrary political power, with little heed paid to their own personal will, but to sacrifice based on their own sense of private obligation, most especially their personal responsibilities to women and children. Even more, putting women at the heart of men's military obligations could also resolve, at least in part, the problem Kathe Kollwitz identified: women gained the courage to let their men serve because men's military service was, in the end, done on behalf of women.

In a particularly creative application of this argument, the historian Robert Westbrook has analyzed the role of the "pinup girl" in the imagination of American soldiers in World War II and how she offered a means for channeling political obligations in gendered form. With the U.S. government and its propaganda machine widely circulating photos of attractive starlets—such as Betty Grable and Rita Hayworth—among the servicemen, the implication seemed to be that if men went to war to defend their country, then defending their country meant fighting for women like Grable and Hayworth. In other words, the "pinup girl" wasn't just about sex (although few could deny that sex was a big part of the pinup's appeal) but about protecting the kinds of women who would also become the loving wives of patriotic servicemen. Thus the stories that circulated about Grable, for example, emphasized her wholesomeness, her "all-Americanness," her marriage in the midst of the war. Sure these women were sexy—and in the age of Freud women exuded a more obvious sexuality than they had previously—but they also epitomized the way of life that American soldiers were fighting for: loving wife, home, family. According to Westbrook, Grable, Hayworth, and other pinup girls performed an essential service in giving a personal and tangible face, not to mention legs, to the more abstract cause of "freedom," or the more intangible problem of defending the state.[4]

Can this argument be extended back into the nineteenth century's Civil War? Where, we might ask, are the pinups of the Civil War era? I can't claim to have found many erotic photos of scantily clad

During World War II, the Office of War Information showcased movie stars as "pinup girls" to help promote the war effort. Here, according to the original OWI caption, Rita Hayworth "sacrificed her bumpers for the duration" of the war, a suggestive reference to Hayworth's promotion of a campaign to turn in metal car parts for war–related needs. (National Archives, Still Picture Records, LICON, Special Media Archives Services Division, College Park, MD)

yet wholesome and virtuous women in the archival folders of Civil War soldiers, although pornography was certainly not unknown to these fighting men of the Victorian era. More to the point, Civil War soldiers frequently carried, if not pinups, then small portrait photographs of sweethearts and wives and other female kin. Indeed, the recent introduction of that photographic innovation known as the carte de visite, so called because it was the size of a traveling card, made it possible for small (and thus highly portable) photographs of women to circulate widely among the men in the ranks. Countless women scraped pennies together in order to be able to have a "likeness" taken that they could send to their menfolk, while countless soldiers did the same for the women left behind. Unlike the Betty Grable pictures, however, sexual content seems to have been minimal. More importantly, cartes de visite were private pictures and not part of any government-sponsored propaganda crusade. Thus, they generally came without a broader, official story regarding soldiers' private obligations, although they certainly could be incorporated into such a narrative. An 1864 illustration, for example, depicted a Union soldier wounded on the battlefield and gazing longingly at the personal portrait from which he derived comfort and inspiration. In this rendering, the soldier became a symbol of Union men everywhere who kept those cartes de visite close to their hearts.

But if propaganda photos were not yet widespread in the middle years of the nineteenth century, Civil War soldiers nonetheless spoke frequently of their civic obligations in private terms, and were often encouraged to do so by their political leaders. Civil War scholar Stephanie McCurry has argued that private and gender-based obligations figured prominently in the leave-taking discourse of Confederate soldiers, especially in the language they spoke early on in the war. Similarly, historian Reid Mitchell has observed that domestic imagery—the metaphor of preserving a family, of punishing errant children—helped many northern soldiers make sense of the political challenges before them in subduing the rebellion. And, like Confederates, Union soldiers also looked to specific mothers, wives, and children to help them make meaningful and tangible a cause

The main photographs of women that would have circulated during the Civil War were not of "pinup girls" but portraits in the form of cartes de visite. This picture shows an unknown woman, possibly a "Mrs. Parker," whose image appeared in Civil War nurse Clara Barton's wartime albums. (Library of Congress, Prints and Photographs Division)

This illustration, "The Dying Soldier," created a sympathetic portrait of the Union soldier who, in his dying moment, casts a loving look at the carte de visite he carries of his family at home. (Library of Congress, Prints and Photographs Division)

that might have otherwise seemed impersonal, even irrelevant, to northern men and their female kin. Indeed, not only did that language make the war intelligible to the soldiers, but it may well have provided a means by which soldiers, as well as government representatives, could persuade women that the reasons for fighting were just, noble, and worthy of their support. "It is for the future welfare of your selfe and children, that causes me to be separated from you," one Ohio soldier wrote to his wife. A North Carolina colonel was even more explicit about placing women at the center of his military enterprise: "So long as we have such wives, mothers, and sisters to fight for so long will this struggle continue until finally our freedom will be acknowledged."[5]

Sentiments such as these could be found not only in the personal correspondence of Yankees and rebels but in the prescriptive literature as well. According to historian Alice Fahs, who has scrutinized the popular literature of the Civil War era, mothers and daughters and sweethearts figured prominently in wartime stories, serving to personalize the soldier's commitment, and to imbue the political cause—of either union or secession—with emotion and sentiment. In countless stories in which young men anguished over their sense of obligation—to stay at home or to serve the country—women occupied central places in the drama and, in various ways, lent their endorsement to military service. Mothers cried but ultimately relinquished their sons and thereby gave men permission to go to war. In a similar vein, sweethearts suffered as they contemplated absent or soon-to-be-absent lovers but—at least as songs and poems suggested —ridiculed and scorned those men who would not serve. Such renderings allowed women, in symbolic fashion, to tell their men that military obligations might temporarily surmount their home-front responsibilities.[6]

These literary and sometimes visual accounts placed women's consent at the core of military service. Women approved, and even demanded, men's enlistment, and so located themselves at the heart of men's obligation to fight. Both northerners and southerners read stories and poems that presented women as the ones who could propel and legitimize the decisions of young men to join the army. A *Harper's Monthly* writer made women's legitimizing role explicit in the 1863 portrait he composed of "the good mother seated at the window from which floats the household flag. . . . The sight of her and her daughters brings the whole country nearer to us, and the great continent seems to rise before us in living personality, and to speak with her voice, and to glow with our affections. The nation seems to live in the person of its queen, and here every patriotic woman does a great deal to animate and impersonate the whole government." Perhaps it wasn't Betty Grable's legs, but here, nonetheless, was a powerful image of the Union's national enterprise symbolized in the figure of a patriotic mother, a figure whose sentimental influence no doubt lent the more conceptual goal of nationhood considerable emotional appeal. In this way, she might inspire men in their fight for women and she might inspire women to be an inspiration to their men.[7]

A similar rhetorical gesture can be seen in the many stories and poems, as well as actual exercises and ceremonies, that linked women with the flag. In both northern and southern communities, women sewed national and regimental flags in the days leading up to a company's departure. Then, in a final send-off ceremony, they would present their patriotic banners to the departing men, thereby blessing the soldiers' work with flags that represented the material embodiments of their labor and their sacrifice. "Only in such gentle ways as this," remarked a speaker in New Orleans with reference to women's flag-making work, "are those of the softer sex permitted to express the deep-hearted sympathies which bind them to their country by bonds as strong as religious faith and enduring forever." Perhaps no woman suggested a stronger link between the flag and female sacrifice than Barbara Frietchie, immortalized in John Greenleaf Whittier's 1863 poem that told of an elderly woman in Frederick, Maryland, who defiantly waved the American flag when Stonewall Jackson's rebel soldiers temporarily occupied her city. Because Frietchie, through her own words (" 'Shoot if you must this old gray head, but spare your country's flag,' she said") and actions, associated

One of the most popular female flag-wavers during the Civil War was the elderly Barbara Frietchie. Based loosely on a series of incidents that occurred during Confederate general Stonewall Jackson's march through Frederick, Maryland, in September 1862, the figure of Frietchie became immortalized in a poem by John Greenleaf Whittier, who called particular attention to Frietchie's protection of the Stars and Stripes. (Library of Congress, Prints and Photographs Division)

herself so directly with the national emblem, fighting for the flag might become less abstract and more personal: it became, at least for Federal troops, a fight for the brave and self-sacrificing women, not unlike the "good mother" called to mind by *Harper's Monthly*.[8]

But while the public culture, of both the Union and the Confederacy, readily employed women and families to make a case for soldiers' military service, how much did the soldiers themselves interpret their political obligations as personal ones? Did personal and private obligations figure as the essential ingredients in motivating men to go to war? In his own discussion of the subject, James McPherson says no, that both northern and southern soldiers frequently offered clear articulations of the political objectives they were fighting for. To some extent, they had to: when family members divided along sectional lines, it became necessary to explain commitments in more explicitly political terms. John Welsh of Virginia railed against his brother James for joining the Republican Party and supporting Lincoln's call to arms, berating him for going against "home, mother, father, and brothers" in his willingness "to sacrifice all for the dear nigger." James, who had moved from Virginia to Illinois, responded that political issues were paramount. "We have to rise in our might as a free independent nation, and demand that law must and shall be respected," he argued, "or we shall find ourselves wiped from the face of the earth." Surely it would have been difficult for James to ground his political obligation in family commitment— with the "home, mother, father, and brothers" he stood accused of deserting.[9]

Even soldiers who did not reject the political perspective of their family members spoke in self-consciously political and ideological terms about their reasons for fighting and did not always imagine their political commitment in the language of domestic sentiment. Sometimes it was necessary to speak of more abstract goals like union, liberty, or self-government, especially with relatives who urged soldiers to reconsider their military service in favor of coming home. But, to bring us to a more critical understanding of gender and its relationship to political obligation in this conflict, I would also argue that a crucial distinction emerged in the way Unionists and Confederates articulated their military responsibility, a distinction that reflected a broader ideological divide between the sections and had important implications for the way traditional notions of gender were deployed and reinforced, and sometimes challenged, in this period of American history. To state the problem directly: my own findings suggest that it was far more common among Confederates to meld the personal and political, indeed to make the private obligation stand in for a larger ideological motive. While Unionists, at times, did the same, especially in the popular literature and propaganda that circulated in the early days of the war, it was far more common for them, especially in their private explanations of why they fought, to separate the private and the political. Historian Reid Mitchell is not wrong when he argues that Union soldiers understood and discussed their soldiering in domesticated terms, but it does seem that Unionists used domestic references very differently from Confederates. For Confederate soldiers, the domestic allusions tended to be direct, immediate, and personal; for Unionists, they were far more general and metaphorical. And, more often than not, northern soldiers explicitly disavowed immediate, domestic motivations. Indeed, the Union soldiers' articulation of their "cause" suggests that the public propaganda of domestic obligation may not have adequately spoken to the mentality of northern men. By pointedly disentangling their political goals from private ones, these soldiers, it seems, readily embraced a political obligation to the state itself. If Confederate soldiers fought for "home," Union men very clearly—and more self-consciously—fought for "country."

This distinction in explaining the "cause" had important implications for women. Because the Confederates placed domestic commitments central to their wartime enterprise, the iconic power of womanhood was deployed much more forcefully in the Confederate imagination than it was in the Union, and women, in effect, were positioned to make a stronger claim on Confederate sympathies. Consequently, Confederate ideology served to activate southern women, sometimes in new ways that broke with traditional gender practices but also in ways that would create an enduring image of the southern white woman as the focal point of the southern struggle. And yet, because Confederate ideology also hinged on traditional gender values of male protection and female subordination, Confederate ideology offered fewer opportunities for southern white women to cast themselves in new roles and positions. In contrast, the Unionist ideology, precisely because it placed the commitment to nation as something outside and above the commitment to the home, opened the door—even in small ways—to new understandings of gender, and new possibilities for women in the public arena.

But, as we shall see, it also opened the door, more explicitly, to the problem of how women would demonstrate their patriotism in a war that was less about defending the home and more about loyalty to the state.

WITH CONFEDERATES FIGHTING to claim independence, and defending themselves against Union invasion, it is not hard to envision how the Confederate enterprise would make considerable use of the language of private and personal obligation in articulating its political cause. "The conviction that they fought for their homes and women," James McPherson argues, "gave many Confederate soldiers remarkable staying power in the face of adversity." But, claims historian Stephanie McCurry, the notion of defending home and family was not simply a product of the South's demand for home rule or the need to defend their section against an invader; it was also an integral component of the antebellum southern worldview. The slave South was invested in a hierarchical and deeply patriarchal view of the social order, a function, explains historian Elizabeth Fox-Genovese, of an economy that was less infused with market relations and dominated more by households and household relationships. With southern production rooted in broadly conceived households —embracing the home and surrounding farms and plantations—the social order reflected the home-based hierarchy that placed white slaveowning men on top. Such men claimed mastery—and what were essentially property rights—over both black slaves and white family members. White men's authority reflected the nature of the antebellum South's economic order—in which southern males oversaw household-based production, a process that did not take them into a wholly separate sphere of the marketplace but kept them in a more unified sphere of home and work.[10]

But the claim of mastery, as McCurry has explained so compellingly, was also available to southern yeomen, even those who never owned slaves. For them, mastery was rooted in their independent standing as freeholding white men who had the power to control the labor of wives and children. Indeed, the laws of coverture cemented the notion of property ownership in marriage by giving married men free and unfettered access to their wives' property, as well as the income derived from that property and whatever wages wives might earn. Such laws were in place all across the United States, but, in the South, these feme covert statutes placed a free white man, even a relatively poor one, above a black male slave, who clearly had no property rights in, or out, of marriage, and who had no right to a legally sanctioned marital union. That understanding of mastery—for both slaveowners and yeoman farmers—thus constituted the essence of southern white men's identity and became a central touchstone of Confederate propaganda aimed at bringing southern yeomen into the ranks of the secession movement and, eventually, the Confederate army. Thus on the eve of South Carolina's secession from the Union, propagandists appealed to southern white men—slaveholder and nonslaveholder alike—to defend those things that defined them as southern white men: the homes, the wives, and the black and white dependents over which they held power. "The aid of every loyal son," wrote the South Carolina politician John Townsend, "is now needed to defend the rights and honor of his political mother, where nestles the home of his wife and children, and where is deposited all his property for their support." As Townsend's appeal suggests, the southern white man's world revolved partly around a political state, but even more fundamentally around the very localized attachments to home, landed property, and personal dependents.[11]

Once the war was under way, countless men in gray demonstrated this conviction in countless statements in which they explained their reasons for fighting. "We have everything to fight for," explained one Richmond soldier in 1863, "our wives, children, land and principles." Others spoke of protecting "the fair daughters of my own native state . . . from Yankee outrage and atrocity," of shielding "the loved ones who call upon me to defend their homes from pillage." Said one Alabama cavalry soldier in an 1863 letter to his fiancée: "If we fail I expect that my own home will be wrested from me, and would not be surprised if my own Cellie did not soon have the vandals at her door to rob and insult her." Indeed, Confederates frequently spoke of defending their women against potential outrages—often conflating the threat from "black Republicans" and black slaves, and repeatedly throwing up the specter of rape. But evidence suggests they may have been less fearful of actual sexual assaults and more concerned about the very real challenge to their property rights in women, their claim to "mastery," that seemed to be at stake if either "black Republicans" or black slaves were successful in destroying the South's social order.[12]

As the historian Stephen Berry argues, such sentiments not only personalized the Confederate soldiers' political mission; they also fulfilled southern expectations regarding honor and manhood. With protection of women placed central in southern expectations regarding manly duties, southern men enthusiastically enlisted (at least in the first half of the war) in the ranks of the Confederacy as a way to prove their masculine fitness. Indeed, says Berry, Stonewall Jackson may have been one of the very few Confederates who pointedly argued that commitment to country must come ahead of devotion to home and family, leading him to deny one soldier's request to return home to a dying wife. More typical, it seems, were the sentiments of Confederate William Nugent, who intoned, "Dear is my country to me, yet dearer far is [the] treasure [I have] in [my] little woman."[13]

The consequences of such sentiments could be profound. On the one hand, southern white women came to occupy a critical place in the Confederate imagination. Politicians and propagandists thrust women into a far more public and prominent position than white women of the South had previously occupied: they established the moral underpinnings of the Confederate struggle; they had the ability to shape the fate and fortunes of the military enterprise; and their suffering would come to be seen as the very embodiment of the Confederate war effort. Indeed, the extent to which southern white women seemed to embody the Confederate cause became almost a truism of Yankee propaganda as northerners widely condemned the "brutal secessionists" and "venomous she-creatures" ruling the South. This notion took on a more sympathetic form in southern hands. It was women, claimed one southern writer in 1863, who stood behind the South's military venture, making the "Confederate soldier a gentleman of honor, courage, virtue and truth, instead of a cut-throat and vagabond." Actual women garnered praise just as much as metaphorical ones. Reflecting on the women he encountered in Petersburg, Virginia, offering sustenance to needy troops, a Confederate soldier asked, "Who would fail to do and dare for their welfare and safety?" And in one of the most well-known tributes to southern female sacrifice, a southern poet and then a southern painter memorialized an incident in which southern white women, aided by slaves, oversaw the funeral and burial of a Confederate officer, Lt. William Latané, killed in one of J. E. B. Stuart's reconnaissance rides around the Union lines. *The Burial of Latané* called attention to all that Confederate soldiers held dear, everything that defined their status as men, and as soldiers: the women, the children, and the slaves who paid homage to them. Even more, the picture highlighted the essential role of white women in the struggle when it located the plantation mistress, who presides over the burial, at the painting's center. In this way, the southern white woman, forced to take center stage because Union soldiers have refused to allow a southern clergyman to pass through their lines, carries the sentimental and emotional weight of the Confederate cause. The Confederacy, not surprisingly, spoke repeatedly of securing women's prayers for the cause; in *The Burial of Latané* they secured those prayers in a particularly prominent way.[14]

There were, of course, other consequences to the Confederate ranking system that elevated southern women to such a high plateau. Although it may not be quite true to say that the South lost the war when it was no longer possible to blend the causes of home and country, it does seem clear that men and women in the Confederacy faced a crisis when the pursuit of the South's military enterprise seemed more and more inconsistent with the goal of protecting women and families. As home-front suffering increased—whether due to Yankee invasion, slave unrest, or chronic shortages—many Confederates wrestled over the conflicting objectives of nation and

Working from an 1864 painting, The Burial of Latané, *composed by William Washington, the engraver A. G. Campbell created an enormously popular print of the same name that circulated widely in the South after the war. The original poem, painting, and subsequent print all paid homage to the central place of women in the Confederate cause. (Virginia Historical Society, Richmond, VA)*

home. Certainly some Confederates, as James Marten has argued, came to believe that being a good man rested on being a loyal and courageous soldier. And in some parts of the South, like Virginia, where women had to contend on a much more regular basis with Yankee incursions, they may have developed a hardened attitude about keeping up the fight. Yet, for soldiers with families outside Virginia, and for those who strongly felt the obligations to manly honor and family protection, it no doubt became increasingly difficult to resist the pleas from women that their presence was required on the home front. "I hope, when you get exchanged," wrote one mother to her imprisoned Confederate son, "you will think, the time past has sufficed for public service, & that your own family require your protection & help." While the consequence of this particular plea remains unknown, we can imagine how an argument like this carried considerable weight among men who had claimed that their foremost reason for fighting was family security.[15]

Additionally, as McCurry has also pointed out, this close melding of politics with private obligations made it far more difficult for Confederates to envision an abstract national enterprise. With white southern men and women repeatedly holding up the centrality of their localized obligations—to families, to homes, to farms—it became that much harder for Confederates to imagine a nation, something that stood above these personal commitments and that might claim—at times—a greater degree of allegiance and loyalty. Certainly, as the voluminous literature on Confederate nationalism suggests, the question of a national vision in the Civil War South remains complicated and contentious. Without question, southern leaders and various elites, including, at times, southern white women, vigorously defended the distinctive cause and character of their nation. Moreover, many white southerners understood and appreciated the romantic nationalism that pervaded early-nineteenth-century Western culture and freely adopted that discourse for their own struggle. Yet evidence also suggests that average men and women across the South faced considerable obstacles in sustaining a vision of Confederate nationalism, especially as long-standing contradictions between aristocracy and democracy bubbled to the surface. The persistent emphasis on home, family, and locality, it seems, also stifled the nationalist imagination of all Confederates and hindered, in particular, the nationalist vision of Confederate women. Compared to their northern counterparts, Confederate women had far fewer opportunities to imagine themselves as part of a national experience and, as we shall see, generally found it difficult to think about their patriotism as anything other than a willingness to defend and sustain their menfolk in their cause.[16]

Finally, we should note that this Confederate call to arms, steeped as it was in long-standing notions of male protection and female submissiveness, served to reinforce traditional notions of gender relationships in the Civil War South. Men pledged themselves to defend and protect women in their determination to fight the Yankees, while women sought to hold men to their promise, made out of an understanding of women's overwhelming dependence on men, to keep them safe and provided for. Of course, by placing women so central to the South's agenda, Confederates did allow women to become more active agents on their own behalf. Indeed, women of both the planter and yeoman classes spoke more often and more forcefully—to public officials as well as to their male kin—to demand that their protection and preservation remain at the heart of the Confederate enterprise. They assumed what McCurry calls new political identities as "soldiers' wives." But while women may have learned to articulate their needs and demands with greater vigor, Confederate ideology offered scant opportunity for southern white women to develop an independent political identity, one that was not wholly dependent on their personal relationship to the men who fought for the South. In short, when southern white women challenged or criticized the Confederate enterprise, their ability to do so rested heavily on establishing a personal connection to a southern man.[17]

Unlike Confederate pronouncements, Union soldiers' explanations as to why they fought consistently refused to blend the causes of home and country together. "Home is sweet and friends are dear," one Union soldier explained, "but what would they all be to let the country go to ruin." These men voiced arguments that differed dramatically from Confederates', repeatedly separating their commitments to home and to nation and frequently placing their obligation to country as something higher and—at least for the moment—more compelling than their obligation to family and home. "Duty prompts me to go," explained a Michigan recruit. "My country first, home and friends next." Indeed, it is striking to hear the words of Union soldiers and imagine the reaction of their female kin. These, after all, were not words designed to secure a stronger emotional commitment from women for the soldiers' cause. "My duties to my country are of more importance now than my duty to you," Julius Skelton wrote to his wife. And few stated the situation more baldly than the soldier who said: "First my God, second my country, third my mother."[18]

To our ears, of course, a third-place ranking might sound rather callous, but few Union soldiers would have thought they were, in any way, neglecting their family duties. Still, as their writings made clear, home and family did not comprise the essence of their cause, or wholly define their commitment to the nation. Indeed, more often than not, soldiers spoke of familial commitments but made temporal distinctions between the immediate family of today and the family— their own as well as others—of the future. "My grandfather fought and risked his life," wrote one Minnesota soldier, "to bequeath to his posterity . . . the glorious Institutions" threatened by the secessionists. Clearly a familial legacy—dating back to the American Revolution—mattered greatly to this soldier. But, he explained to his wife, he was willing to continue the fight, despite wounds and physical exhaustion, not just for the sake of his immediate family, "but also for the sake of the country's millions who are to come after us."[19]

These frequent references to "future welfare," "future prosperity," and those "who are to come after us" suggest that Union soldiers had trained their sights on an objective that stood beyond their immediate families and had much to do with the nation, and the government, that would help ensure their family's well-being. Imagining their own families linked up with future, yet still unknown, families seemed to be one way in which northern soldiers envisioned a national community, that "horizontal comradeship" referred to by Benedict Anderson in his study of modern nationalism. Like Anderson's nation, this was an imagined community that had clear political and geographic boundaries, rested on notions of simultaneity, and was positioned on a forward- and backward-looking time frame. Yet Union soldiers also spoke of and embraced a national enterprise in less metaphorical ways, pointedly separating that national entity from anything private or personal. Why were these men so forceful in declaring their obligation to a relatively abstract national entity? Certainly the fact that Union soldiers were leaving their states and their communities to make war in a (relatively) far-off locale must have encouraged them to think about their fight in more intangible ways. "We are fighting for matters real and tangible," a Texas soldier explained, "our property and our homes." The Yankee struggle, in contrast, was about "matters abstract and intangible." Moreover, unlike the Confederates who had to envision, at least to some extent, a brand new national enterprise, Unionists could more easily imagine their fight as one to preserve a long-standing political tradition and historic political institutions. And while Confederates, too, made recourse to the principles of the founding fathers, Unionists, it seems, could more easily make the link from the political struggles of their forefathers to a concrete political experiment that had lasted through 1860 and that they fought to preserve. As the Minnesota soldier quoted above explained, his "grandfather fought and risked his life to bequeath to his posterity . . . the glorious Institutions" that now must be preserved from the rebels. The preservation of an already existing government, in other words, could, in fact, make the Union soldiers' political objectives seem more concrete and tangible than the Confederate soldiers' objective of creating something new and untested.[20]

But aside from the historical and political imperatives of the moment, I would also argue that the readiness with which Union soldiers separated their commitment to the home from, and subordinated it to, their obligation to the nation revealed the distinctive ideological framework of the antebellum North and the unique socioeconomic world that had been created by the early nineteenth century's market and industrial revolutions. The dramatic economic changes that affected the antebellum Northeast, although they did not signal the emergence of a fully industrialized economy, did mean that a higher premium was placed on income and wealth derived from profitable, as opposed to subsistence-oriented, enterprises. Those economic changes, moreover, had significant consequences in terms of gender relations and the ways that northern men and women defined their notions of manhood and womanhood. Increasingly, northern men turned away from the home—toward banks, stores, workshops, and other places of economic exchange—in order to make their income, while the world of the home, and its never-ending array of tasks, was increasingly associated with women. This notion of the "separate spheres" was not a true reflection of the way all northern men and women lived their lives, but it was a powerful ideological construction that spoke to genuine changes that many Americans had experienced while also positing a natural and morally beneficial demarcation of society based on gender. Even more, as the historian Jeanne Boydston has observed, because women's work in the home produced no tangible economic wealth, that is, no cash income, northerners in the antebellum era tended to take a somewhat diminished view of the home's significance. Certainly as the domestic literature of the period implied, the home had immense emotional and sentimental appeal. But, when measured by the wealth-creating standard of the day, the home also clearly occupied a secondary role, as a place that had less to do with productive, masculine toil and more to do with ethereal, feminine "leisure."[21]

All this suggests that men who came from the North on the eve of the Civil War had already embraced a worldview that was significantly different from the worldview of most white southerners, especially on the question of male and female spheres. While white southern men identified themselves as the masters of a broadly conceived home, northern men separated the home from the "outside world," associated men's work—both political and economic—with the demands and pressures of that "outside world" beyond the home, and viewed the so-called woman's sphere of home and family as a subordinate sphere in the overall scheme of things. Even more, as Boydston has persuasively argued, the antebellum northern man's sense of identity and manhood rested less on the patriarchal claim of the father who passed on material wealth and property for future generations and more on his ability to earn an income that would support his family in the present: to be, in the parlance of the day, the family "breadwinner." Unlike white southern men, whose very being was bound up with their status as family patriarchs who controlled the property that would be passed on to succeeding generations, northern men turned their sights to a sphere that stood largely outside the world of women, the home, and the family.[22]

The separate spheres ideology, then, helped accustom Union soldiers to the "nation over home" discourse of the Civil War era. It gave men a sense of a world, a "horizontal community," that stood outside the immediate boundaries of domestic life. It also introduced northern men to the idea that, in order to provide for their families, they must leave the family for the "outside" world of the marketplace or, in this case, the battlefield. In addition, Union men, more so than Confederates, felt comfortable with the idea of subordinating one sphere—women's—to the demands of another. "My absence from home is, of course, a source of grief to Lida and the children," wrote one Union man from Kentucky to his sister, "but an all-absorbing, all-engrossing sense of duty, alike to country and family, impelled me." In a similar fashion, Iowa soldier Taylor Peirce also tried to keep family central to his sense of obligation, but by envisioning that responsibility in terms of his family's *future* welfare he also suggested that he could not be guided by immediate personal imperatives and looked toward a more abstract objective. "Dear Catherine," Peirce explained to his wife, "the happiness and prosperity of our Children depend on the Suppression of this rebellion and although you know that I love you and the children as well a man can and will probably have more concern for your present welfare than most men yet your future prosperity is of greater importance than anything else in the world." In this way, Peirce certainly never abandoned, in his mind, his private duties; yet he filtered his personal commitments through a political prism in a way that Confederate soldiers generally did not. By invoking the idea of "future prosperity" Peirce conveyed his commitment to the nation's security and, thus, to the means by which his family's well-being and success would be ensured. For Peirce, in other words, it was the nation that made the home and the family meaningful, whereas for Confederates it was home and family that gave the idea of nation any kind of significance.[23]

The willingness of Union soldiers like Peirce to identify an abstract nation-state as a source of "future prosperity" might, in fact, indicate that the nation-state, at least as it was experienced by most northerners in the antebellum era, wasn't as abstract as we might imagine. A state that could secure "prosperity" for its subjects, after all, might manifest itself in peoples' lives in very tangible ways. Although pre–Civil War America was characterized, in all sections of the country, by the absence of a well-developed state apparatus, far more northerners, male and female, would have been the beneficiaries of some state-supported social welfare services than southerners. Consider, for example, the situation with respect to public education. In 1850, the white population in the northern states was more than double what it was in the slaveholding South, yet these states had more than three times as many public schools and twenty times as many public libraries. By and large, southern states failed to invest in public improvement to the degree that northern states did. The result was not only a higher rate of illiteracy in the South (7.4 percent among southern whites as opposed to 2 percent among northern whites) but perhaps, too, less reason to feel connected to a political state that stood above and outside the home. In contrast, a larger percentage of northern men and women on the eve of the Civil War would have experienced the material benefits of the state apparatus in the form of public schooling. They would have also been exposed, along the way, to a greater degree of nationalistic patriotism that found its way into textbooks and public school rituals.[24]

Girls as well as boys had benefited from the Yankee pledge to public schools, a fact that might also help explain the extent to which northern women made their own commitment to the national enterprise. Certainly, the separation of home and country placed a difficult challenge before Union women, much different than the one that female Confederates encountered. If they accepted the goals and objectives of the war, Union women also had to accept that the Union cause was not about home and family, and that home and family must, in fact, take a backseat to the present military and political imperatives. It was a challenge that many women, albeit reluctantly, accepted. Grace Weston wrote to her fiancé from Chicago and accepted the national imperative that compelled him to enlist. "If you do your duty to your country," she wrote to him in January 1864, "we shall have a right to such a home under the 'starry banner' and we cannot but be happy in the consciousness of duty faithfully performed." Like Taylor Peirce, Grace Weston believed that domestic happiness would come, but only after national duty had taken precedence. Eliza Otis, a resident of Louisville, Kentucky, whose husband, Harrison, enlisted immediately after the attack on Sumter, also learned to reconcile herself to the new priorities that placed nation before home. "It's hard to do without him," she confided in her diary, "and yet I would as soon lay my head upon the block, and throw away forever my hopes of immortality, as to say one word to dissuade him from duty, or lead him to seek a life of inglorious ease at home, in this hour of our Nation's imminent peril. His country," she added significantly, "has higher claims upon him now than I have."[25]

Such remarks were by no means typical of the views of all northern women. As was true in the Confederacy, many, many female Unionists told their husbands and sweethearts, especially as the war began to take a greater toll on human life, just how difficult it was to give them up for the fight, how much they longed to have them home, and how they thought it was time to make homes and families a priority once again. Such sentiments may have been more widespread in the border regions and lower Midwest where antiwar Democrats had gained a degree of political prominence. I hope you "stay until you have seen one great battle, & done as much after it as you can possibly do, & then I would like to have you come home to stay," wrote Ohio resident Ann Cotton to her army surgeon husband, Josiah. Such pleas, however, never gained quite the power that similar pleas from southern white women did. This may, in part, have to do with the relative lack of suffering that women endured on the northern home front, the fact that few northern communities experienced enemy invasions and crippling shortages or had little to fear in terms of slave insubordination. Yet, since, I think, people rarely reconcile themselves to their own suffering by comparing their lot with those who suffer more, other explanations also played a part. More specifically, I believe the manner in which the Union cause had so often been articulated, as a battle that did not so much meld the private and the political but one that made the political objective of saving the nation-state a distinctive, and elevated, goal in and of itself, meant that northern women's requests to have men come home could never assume as much force as similar requests assumed in the South. Stated another way, I believe that Union men had a language, and a vision, one that women sometimes came to share, that made it easier for them to insist that domestic demands must be (and would have to remain for the duration of the war) subordinate to national ones.[26]

Let me consider in some detail one particularly interesting Civil War couple—Elizabeth and James Bowler—to illustrate this point. Born in Maine in 1838, James Bowler moved to the Minnesota territory at the age of nineteen. He worked as a printer and then as a teacher, meeting his sweetheart, Lizzie Caleff, when he taught school in the town of Nininger in 1859 and 1860. Despite objections from Lizzie's father, the couple soon became engaged, only to have military hostilities intrude on their romantic bliss. Upon the Civil War's outbreak, James Bowler enlisted with the First Minnesota Regiment, Company E.

Lizzie and James wrote often to one another while James was at war. Lizzie, in particular, wrote often of her longing to see James back at home. In his letters to Lizzie, James acknowledged that he, too, wished to see his fiancée again but also repeatedly explained that he did not want to return until the "great object" for which the war had commenced had been accomplished, with the rebellion put down once and for all. In September of 1862 James was temporarily reassigned from his post in the South to his home state of Minnesota, to help put down the uprising of the Sioux Indians. Now, writing to Lizzie to explain why he had to follow through on this military assignment and could not take leave to visit her, James seemed to struggle with the language of political and private

James Bowler, of Nininger, Minnesota, posed in his Union army uniform with his bride, Elizabeth Caleff, also of Nininger, shortly after the two were married late in 1862. (Minnesota Historical Society)

obligations. "Next to my duty to God," he explained, in what seems, at first, to be a typical restatement of the Union soldiers' ranking system, "comes my duty to my country and its suffering, unfortunate people who have become victims of the enemies of God and humanity." James thus maintained his commitment to "country" as an objective he placed above home and family, although his new assignment, being back in Minnesota to put down an Indian revolt, posed new challenges for James when it came to explaining his military obligation. Describing the threat the Sioux posed to homes and families, James here departed from the usual Union philosophy and more pointedly blended the private with the political, explicitly making women, like Lizzie, the objects of his obligation. "Did you ever," he asked Lizzie, "contemplate how horrible it is that young, respectable females like yourself and your friends are in the hands of savages who have not the least restraint, either moral or physical, upon their conduct toward their victims?" Subduing this Native

American attack on his home soil, in other words, prompted James to articulate his political obligations in private terms, perhaps to drive home to Lizzie why, despite his proximity to her, he still could not see her.[27]

Yet, in fighting the Confederacy, James worked to keep his political objectives free from private and domestic restraints. Indeed, he had to focus more intently on keeping his priorities straight after the fall of 1862—when he and Lizzie were married—and then again after the fall of 1863 when Lizzie gave birth to their daughter. As childbirth neared and then as she faced the challenge of raising their child alone, Lizzie kept up a steady refrain requesting that James leave the army and return to Minnesota. James, however, explained that although he appreciated the new and even more compelling domestic demands he faced, he had always made his main concern clear. "It has been my intention all along," he wrote to Lizzie in September of 1864, "to remain in the army until the end of this war. . . . I do not wish to be compelled to leave the army until I can see fully and clearly that we have a country in which we can live in peace and security." In the end, James Bowler remained in the army even after the conflict had ended, serving as a major with the 113th U.S. Colored Infantry in Arkansas until 1866. His ability to do so, I would argue, rested in part on the way he—and other Unionists—had made their political—and national—cause clearly paramount to, and disentangled from, a private protection of homes and families. Drawing on a language that Confederate soldiers generally lacked, Union men could resist the notion that women and families must come first.[28]

Lizzie Bowler, for one, struggled mightily with those priorities, although even she stayed abreast of the war news and learned to reconcile herself to her husband's absence. She also pointed out to James that, as a Canadian by birth, her allegiance to the Union was naturally somewhat qualified. But while Lizzie Bowler maintained a lukewarm patriotism toward her adopted homeland, other Union women made a self-conscious decision to accept the subordination of domestic concerns to national ones. "For any thing else I could not let you go," the fiancée of a navy officer explained, "but . . . I am glad dear that I can give something for my country." Because Union men made it clear that they fought for "country," Union women recognized that the hardship they endured, when their male kin went to serve, was also for country. Unlike Confederate women, they would have found it difficult to rationalize their sacrifice as something that placed their own security and protection as the centerpiece of military obligation. Instead, they, just like Union men, had to reckon with the elevation of national obligation over home. "I feel it is a duty I owe my country," Emeline Ritner of Iowa explained in a letter to her soldier-husband in 1864, "to give up my dear friends to fight and even this in her defense."[29]

To a great extent, of course, the Unionists, men and women, who made these kinds of calculations about the competing claims of family and nation were white. For African American men and women, the mix of personal and political motivations reflected the complicated state of antebellum racial politics. Whether they lived in the South or the North, free or slave, black men and women essentially had no nation to which they could lay claim when the war began. According to the *Dred Scott* decision of 1857, they had no rights as citizens in any state in the union. And, prior to 1863, black men could not fight—in any official capacity—for a country, regardless of the patriotic attachments they may have harbored. Indeed, Confederate leaders recognized, to some extent, the problem of their slaves' political alienation, given the fact that slave men possessed neither homes nor families under the slave regime. Thus, to the extent that the Confederacy sought to recruit slave men to the Confederate cause, and prevent them from giving aid and assistance to the Union, they made a corresponding acknowledgment of the need to give those men a domestic stake in the southern enterprise, that is, to make them free. "Let them be declared free, placed in the ranks, and told to fight for their homes and country," argued one Confederate journal. Ultimately, of course, the Confederacy failed to fully implement this plan, recognizing no doubt that it would cost them the support of white men who counted slaves as part of the domestic property they fought to defend.[30]

On the northern side of the conflict, especially as the Union struggle became more clearly linked with the struggle for slave emancipation, the conditions were considerably better for the military recruit-
ment of slave men, as well as northern free black men, and for
securing an attachment, on the part of the black community, to the
nation. Slaves in the South increasingly identified with the symbols
and representatives of the United States as the nation increasingly
took up the cause of the slaves. Even more, in taking up the cause of
the slaves, the Union struggle also, in a very direct and personal
way, became a struggle for black homes and black families, institutions that had been rendered meaningless in a slave regime. Thus
Union officials, along with northern missionaries recruited to the
cause, made it a priority to instruct contraband communities in the
Union-occupied South about marital relations and domestic comforts, while simultaneously imparting lessons in patriotism. In this
way, enslaved men and women were encouraged to see their future—
including their ability to enjoy and feel secure in their attachment to
homes and families—as bound to the efforts of the U.S. government
and the U.S. Army. This mix of patriotic and personal motivations
propelled tens of thousands of former slaves, as well as free black
men, into the Union ranks after black enlistment began in 1863.[31]

Yet the national struggle for Union and the personal struggle for
homes and families did not blend seamlessly for southern slaves.
Slave men and women frequently found their commitment to the
Federal cause tried and tested, especially in those moments when the
nation revealed itself to be largely insensitive to black family life. In
this regard, black men balked at the idea of ranking nation higher
than home if the nation showed only callous disregard for black
women and black families. For them, it was a question not of demonstrating any kind of "mastery" over women and children but about
making a break from the oppressive conditions of slavery. Black
soldiers in Virginia complained bitterly that their service for the
Union made them feel like slaves, especially because it exposed their
wives and their children to poverty, starvation, and abuse, including
abuse from Union soldiers themselves. Although his wife was not

abused, black soldier George Washington wrote to Lincoln to request a discharge, explaining that since he had not yet received any pay from the Union administration, he had to return home to care for his wife and children. For Washington, in other words, it wasn't a question of ranking nation higher than home but rather fearing that, in fighting for the nation, he had jeopardized his home. If the nation seemed unable and unwilling to protect black families, it only served to make black men and women, especially the former slaves, more reluctant about their support for the nation's cause.[32]

Of course, white Unionists, too, questioned their patriotism when their country left women and children exposed and impoverished. Women who lived in New York City in July 1863 would have argued that it was precisely the suffering of their neglected families that led them to protest the Lincoln administration's attempt to draft their men into the Union army. Indeed, throughout the North hundreds of thousands of men and women resisted the draft, although most registered their opposition in less dramatic fashion than the New York City rioters. Many would have explained their right to resist by pointing to familial duties: the need to care for ailing parents, to support wives and young children, to continue to be the family breadwinner. In fact, because it was so difficult to explain the Union cause as an obligation to protect homes and families, the appeal to stay out of the military for the sake of the family surely carried considerable weight with many northerners. Recent research on the subject of northern draft deserting and resisting has thus reversed the assessment of an earlier generation of scholars who believed such activity was minimal: instead, new findings suggest that many northerners were not persuaded to relinquish their traditional duties to home and family for the demand to safeguard the nation.[33]

Recognizing how difficult it could be to convince men to subordinate their familial responsibilities to the Union cause, federal and state officials took a number of steps to underscore the tangible and material benefits associated with their version of the nation-state, especially to secure the patriotic support of non-elite northerners. At the local, state, and federal levels, government officials all participated, although with varying degrees of effectiveness, in assuming the work of male protection. Various states made regular monthly payments to the wives and children of enlisted men, with northern cities sometimes supplementing this even further. The state of Wisconsin, for example, gave soldiers' wives $5 per month while children received $2 each. In April of 1861, the city council of Philadelphia voted funds for the families of departing volunteers, providing an average distribution per family of about $1.50 per week. In the South, such assistance was far less extensive and consistent and generally came from private, as opposed to public, relief efforts. In part this reflected the stronger tax base that northern governments had at their disposal and enhanced bureaucratic mechanisms for distributing funds. In any event, it certainly seems likely that northern state governments, as well as the federal government, further secured the support of civilians and soldiers to the cause of nationhood by expanding the kind of social welfare functions—like public education—that had given greater meaning to antebellum northerners' patriotic loyalties.

Perhaps the ultimate expression of this idea came when, in July of 1862, the federal government formalized and expanded its system of providing pensions for wives, children, and even mothers and sisters who had been dependent on a soldier now deceased. Under the new pension law, those women who filed legitimate claims now received regular monthly payments for themselves and for dependents. Even more, the new system was, in its own way, an acknowledgment of the Union soldier's separation of private and public obligations and a recognition that the protection of women and families was, to a great extent, no longer simply a private matter to be left in the hands of individual husbands and fathers. If soldiers like Taylor Peirce had pledged themselves to the "future prosperity" of their wives and their families, the pension program seemed to provide a tangible manifestation of how loyalty to the nation-state could translate into at least some measure of security, if not actual "prosperity." And, with the new pension system in place, the state recognized an obligation to shoulder some of Union men's domestic burdens, a not insignificant development in light of the commitment that Union men had made when they ranked nation higher than home.[34]

In contrast, southern society, both before and during the war, tended to emphasize the individual man's protection of his own female relatives and thus hesitated to relinquish the job of male protection to a government bureaucracy. Indeed, when poor Richmond women, many claiming to be the kin of Confederate soldiers, took to the streets of their city in April of 1863, demanding that government officials allow them to buy flour and other necessities at government prices, instead of at exorbitant market rates, they found very little sympathy from Confederate officials. In part, this reflected elite southerners' traditional disregard for lower-class suffering, but it also suggested that the southern notion of male protection rested, for the most part, within the limited and immediate parameters of family life, perhaps extending occasionally to notions of neighborly support but rarely to the level of government aid.[35]

BUT IF CONFEDERATE IDEOLOGY consistently reinforced traditional gender practices, the Union ideology may have opened the door to subtle departures from tradition. Indeed, if wives and mothers and sisters figured less centrally as the Union soldiers' objects of obligation, it could also become possible to expect women to do more to fend for themselves, perhaps even to assume greater authority over matters they did not usually oversee. Thus we saw how Taylor Peirce, after his enlistment with the Twenty-second Iowa Volunteer Infantry in August of 1862, explained to his wife, Catherine, that his military obligations made it impossible for him to make the present welfare of his wife and children a priority. But if Peirce believed it necessary, for the time being, to relinquish some of his immediate breadwinning responsibilities, he nonetheless hoped that his wife could step in and, at least partly, fill his shoes. "I want thee to take hold and do for thyself," Taylor explained, "and use thy own judgment about matters and lirn to lean on thyself so that If I should be called away thee will have a knowledge of business to make a living for thyself." He thus urged her to make decisions on her own about selling his sawmill and keeping their finances in order, logical consequences of his waging a war for something that went beyond home protection. Sam Evans communicated a similar message, although with far less decorum, to a female cousin. "You need not be uneasy about starving where there is ground to till and you keep your health. It is no disgrace to work." Might a Confederate soldier have used similar language with an unhappy female relative? Perhaps, but his words would have undermined the idiom of patriarchal protection so central to antebellum southern thinking and to the Confederate war effort.[36]

And while they were sometimes reluctant to assume too much official responsibility, women themselves often acknowledged the need to go beyond their traditional duties when they sorted through bank accounts, butchered hogs, sold their crops and other merchandise, or supervised employees. Union ideology may have made it easier for men, and sometimes for women, too, to challenge, even slightly, traditional gender practices—including women's long-standing isolation from most financial responsibilities—precisely because a traditional understanding of gender obligations had not been made so central to the larger military obligations that Union soldiers embraced. If, as Union soldiers explained, nation ranked higher than home, then women must be prepared to do whatever was necessary to allow their male kin to keep those priorities in order. Thus when Fanny Pierce of Weymouth, Massachusetts, wrote to her brother Elliot, she tried to convey her determination to assume a new level of responsibility for domestic affairs. Explaining that the interest on their mortgage was coming due, Fanny suggested that she could "raise ten dollars of it in time and perhaps a little more, but feel a little anxious about the rest and thought I had better mention it to you, knowing you would like to help if it was in your power." In the end, though, she didn't want this type of obligation to constrain her sibling in any way from his more demanding duties. "I think," she concluded, "you have enough to bear already. Don't bother yourself now."[37]

Finally, there was yet one other way that the Union mentality encouraged women to break away from traditional patterns of gender behavior. Because they were being called upon to give up their men for something higher than home, women, as we have seen, had to recognize that their own sacrifices, as women, involved the preservation of the nation. While Confederate ideology encouraged women to personalize and domesticate the Confederate cause, Union women had to embrace the subordination of domestic ideals to national ones. Such thinking could spur women to ponder more deeply what the sacrifice for nation and country—as a separate entity—actually meant. Subtle evidence exists that women, throughout the Union, were beginning to think along these lines. Quite a few began thinking more about local and national politics. A few even made the critical leap from recognizing their husbands' and fathers' commitment to "their" country to embracing a joint commitment to fight for "our" country. The wife of an Ohio sergeant made this point explicitly. "Your country's cause," she explained to her husband, "is my cause." Grace Weston encouraged her fiancé to serve with similar sentiments: "I can never weary of good and noble purposes and have never for a moment doubted that you were sincere in your desire to serve your, our true country." Certainly one could find southern white women expressing themselves in similar ways, telling of their commitments to their cause and their country. Yet I would argue that northern women's expressions reflected more deeply considered ideas and could be found, I believe, amongst a more economically and socially diverse range of women and not just those of the elite. And, as was true with Union men, northern women's expressions of patriotism also reflected a more self-conscious disentangling of the cause of "home" from the cause of "country." As we shall see, the Union struggle eventually forced northern women to give greater consideration to the political meaning they attached to their loyalty and their patriotism, especially when—in the middle of the Civil War—northern women's patriotism came under increasingly sharp attack.[38]

The Problem of Women's Patriotism, North and South

IF THE CIVIL WAR prompted numerous references to "founding fathers" among Union and Confederate soldiers, so did it also stimulate much talk about "founding mothers" for women on both sides of the conflict. While soldiers looked to the principles and practices of the revolutionary generation as validation for their present course of action, women likewise looked to the founding mothers as a template on which they could model their own wartime participation. Two weeks after the attack on Fort Sumter, one woman wrote to the New York *Herald* urging northern women to do their part for the war, appealing to the "blood of '76" that coursed through female veins. A Mississippi lieutenant encouraged his wife to "Think of our Revolutionary mothers daily." And a southern songwriter used a similar reference point in urging Confederate women to let their male kin go to war. "Our Mothers," the lyricist explained, "Did So before Us." Throughout the course of the Civil War both northern and southern women would look frequently to the women of the revolutionary era for some source of inspiration: as models of economic sacrifice; as organizers of consumer boycotts; and, perhaps most importantly, as women who bravely sent their sons and husbands and brothers to face the cannons of war.[1]

The fact that the legacy of revolutionary-era women could be called upon in so many different capacities might suggest to us that the American Revolution did not bequeath to the women, or men, of the Civil War era a clear-cut model of what female sacrifice and patriotism meant. As the historian Linda Kerber has suggested, female patriotism was a troubling concept at the time of the American Revolution and remained so for quite some time. Indeed, the word itself—rooted in the Greek designation for father—posed an obvious contradiction for women. While Enlightenment philosophers tackled issues of patriotism, and the patriotic demands a republic placed upon its citizens, they made little headway in clarifying the contradictory nature of women's national allegiance. Republicanism, as it was formulated by theorists of the seventeenth and eighteenth centuries, privileged the position of the male heads of household—and assumed that such men, who also had economic control over their wives and daughters, were the rightful political representatives of their families. Consequently, most republican thinkers subscribed to the belief that women naturally had, as one commentator explained, "less patriotism than men" because they could only relate to the country indirectly through their relationships with husbands, fathers, and sons.[2]

The revolutionary experience, as Kerber herself has argued, did not fundamentally alter this notion of subordinated patriotism. True, women often subscribed to a more active idea of national allegiance, going beyond the passive work of simply letting men go. And some women, notably Abigail Adams, believed that because women remained above partisanship and political careerism, "patriotism in the female sex" stood on a higher moral platform than men's. Still, women's presence in the ranks of both Tories and Patriots prompted some in the early republic to question just how deep women's patriotic commitment to the American cause had been, apparently ignoring the fact that men, too, could be found on both sides of the conflict. Even more significantly, it seems the Revolution did little to advance the notion that women might have a political identity distinct from male kin, and thus have the capacity for an autonomous expression of patriotism. Right after the Revolution, American courts upheld the view that married women could not be held to an oath of loyalty because—by definition—they must follow the political beliefs of their husbands. Women's patriotism, in other words, could only be reflected in a woman's support for male kin and not as a manifestation of her independent civic allegiance.[3]

The predominant view of female patriotism continued, through the antebellum era, to deny women any autonomous political identity, although the emergence of the early women's rights movement in the 1840s and 1850s did suggest that some "strong-minded" women might reject that standard of behavior. But most Americans living at the time of the Civil War would, no doubt, have adhered to some version of Montesquieu's belief that women in a republic lay claim to patriotism precisely (and, as some saw it, exclusively) in sending men off to fight because doing so meant that women recognized that their private claim (always women's priority) would rank lower than the public claim of the state. Here, then, was the essence of female sacrifice: to put aside what was assumed to be their domestic focus and to give their support to men's public and political obligations. Such was the sentiment articulated by "Kate," the heroine of a *Harper's Weekly* short story written in 1864, who accepted the marriage proposal offered to her by her soldier sweetheart. "You are my soldier now," she told her fiancé, "Mine to send out into the battle-field to dream of and to pray for. . . . I have always repined that I had no gift for my country, now I can give my best and dearest to aid her cause." These were the words, too, uttered by a Virginia mother to her enlisting son, and as reported by a Virginia newspaper. "Your country calls. . . . I am ready to offer you up in defense of your country's rights and honor." Here was a model, North and South, for women to emulate.[4]

But exceptions could be found, and in fact with increasing frequency after the war was under way. There were some women who broke with family loyalties and thus had to make some independent determinations about their patriotism. Catherine Edmondston of South Carolina parted ways with her sisters and mother and even her father, although not her husband, in declaring her support for secessionist principles. The Union, she believed, was "no longer glorious. . . . When it ceases to be voluntary, it degenerates into a hideous oppression." More alarming, still, were women, Confederate sympathizers in the North and Union sympathizers in the South, who clearly stood outside the parameters of proper female behavior, especially when they acted alone and made public demonstrations of their political sympathies. As the historian Elizabeth Varon has demonstrated, female spies—like Rose Greenhow in Washington, DC, and Elizabeth Van Lew in Richmond, Virginia—posed serious challenges to the dominant assumptions regarding women's lack of political independence and the traditional notion that patriotic women simply supported their menfolk. When the Union press acknowledged that even women, like Greenhow, might aid the enemy and could not be protected by presumptions of female innocence, it became clear that the war would breach some of the barricades regarding women's patriotism. Still, women like Greenhow and Van Lew tended to be shunned, at least by their enemies, as aberrations of the dominant norm. Clearly neither had adhered to the rules regarding women's political behavior as explained by the editor of *Leslie's Monthly* who saw the war, for both northern and southern ladies, not as "a question of politics, but [as] a question of home, of father, husband, brother or lover." "Naturally," *Leslie's* editor insisted, they both "share the enthusiasm and devotion of those in whose judgment they are accustomed to confide."[5]

This notion that women lacked an independently patriotic perspective was, I think, especially pronounced in the South. Southern women had little experience with the nascent women's rights movement; and southern society, due to its profoundly patriarchal orientation, tended to be even less hospitable than the North to expressions—either politically, economically, or socially—of female autonomy. Moreover, the notion of women's independent patriotism was further limited in the South by the parameters of Confederate ideology. Because Confederate thinking rested so strongly on the intertwining of nation and home, the nationalism that both Confederate men and women subscribed to was, inherently, circumscribed. Like their men, southern white women were called on to support a cause that put female protection and traditional domestic concerns at its heart. "A nation fighting for its own homes and liberty," remarked Louisianan Kate Stone in 1861, "cannot be overwhelmed." And Sarah Espy echoed words that had been uttered countless times by Confederate men when she prayed that, above all else, "the women and children of the South be saved from their Northern murderers."[6]

Which is not to suggest that there was no understanding of a Confederate national enterprise or an appeal to an abstract political state, or that even women didn't, in their own way, reckon with a more intangible articulation of Confederate nationalism. Yet, as historian Drew Faust has observed, the process of defining the distinctive nature of the southern nation posed certain irreconcilable tensions. In order to justify the Confederacy's separation from the Union, Confederate officials had to highlight the institution of slavery; but highlighting slavery meant, in turn, the potential alienation of the southern white nonslaveowning majority. Indeed, in the course of the war, that alienation became more and more manifest as nonslaveowners expressed their opposition to numerous government actions, including the conscription laws that forced men of a certain age to serve the Confederacy but exempted some who owned slaves. Confederate officials also refused, on a number of occasions, to come to the aid of poorer women and families to relieve them from price-gouging and the general impoverishment brought on by wartime suffering. All this impinged on nonslaveowning whites' ability to identify themselves with a broader "imagined community" of the

Confederate nation. Such practices also, no doubt, compelled many white southerners to insist that if the manly protection of the home was, indeed, central to the Confederate enterprise and if the Confederacy itself made only a marginal—if not negative—contribution to that objective, then surely the imperative to serve the Confederate cause was greatly diminished.[7]

As we've seen, Unionists made a different calculation regarding the relationship between home and nation. Union soldiers repeatedly prioritized their fight for the national government over the fight for homes and families. What did these differing ways of prioritizing home and country mean for the way Union and Confederate women came to understand their commitments in wartime? If they proclaimed loyalty to the cause, to what were they loyal? And, if they accepted the priorities made by Union men, were Union women loyal simply to what their men proclaimed, or to something beyond their own domestic commitments? My focus, in this chapter, rests more with the Union than with the Confederacy because I believe the conditions that informed the North's discussion of gender and patriotism laid the foundation for a more significant break with traditional notions of women's subordinated loyalty. The Union struggle increasingly prompted northern women, and some men, to question long-standing models of female political behavior, ultimately encouraging northern women to see themselves as individuals who related to the nation-state, not indirectly through male family members, but on their own, independent, terms.

IN THE EARLY DAYS OF THE WAR, women on both sides of the sectional divide threw themselves into "patriotic" work, taking on tasks and adopting an orientation toward the work that revealed significant similarities. North and South, women gathered first informally and then in more structured societies to encourage enlisting soldiers, to sew banners and flags for departing troops, to prepare packages of supplies to be shipped to soldiers in camp and in the field, and to hold fairs and benefits for the purpose of raising money to buy necessary provisions. The organizations bore similar names, differentiated only by geographic locale: the "Philadelphia Ladies' Aid Society," the "Haverhill and Bradford Soldiers' Relief Society," the "Ladies Soldiers Aid Society of Natural Bridge, Virginia." South and North, these organizations, along with women's early support efforts, also elicited similar tributes from male leaders, pleased to see women engaged in the traditional patriotic work of humbly supporting men's military efforts. Two weeks after the fall of Sumter, the New York *Herald* offered the kind of praise that Confederate journals would have echoed: they hailed "the enthusiasm of the women" and applauded their determination to "appear on the battlefield not in the character of an Amazon, but as an angel of mercy." Thus both northern and southern commentators hoped to discourage inappropriate demonstrativeness on the part of their women; and both praised "women" as a universal and unified group of loyal participants. Indeed, the appeal to universal "womanhood" was at least partially driven by a desire, in both sections, to mute potentially divisive class tensions. The expectation of and applause for "female" selflessness suggested that throughout society, regardless of social class, women would be called upon to sacrifice, and that men, also regardless of social class, would be able to avail themselves of that feminine, and appropriately submissive, devotion.[8]

In both sections, too, women were often buoyed, at least initially, by the soldiers' aid work. They enjoyed gathering with female friends and neighbors and took solace in feeling useful and productive. Interestingly, women in both sections were also struck by a feeling of solidarity that had taken hold among women as they gathered in these support efforts. In Boston in May of 1861, the well-to-do Elizabeth Rogers Cabot found the people of the North "splendidly united" and observed "something beautiful in the way everybody is at work in the same cause." That same month, plantation mistress Catherine Edmondston found the same to be true in South Carolina. "Never was known such unanimity of action amongst all classes," she remarked. Perhaps for both women there was, indeed, the appearance of unanimity as they participated in gatherings that linked them, in new and unfamiliar ways, with women not in their immediate social circle. It seems likely, however, that in both Cabot's and Edmondston's societies, women of the poorest classes were not fully united in the efforts and that the perceived "unanimity" reflected a fairly limited spectrum of those from the middle and upper classes.[9]

Still, whether directed toward the Union or the Confederate military effort, ladies' aid work ultimately compelled women to challenge some of the most traditional assumptions about female patriotism, especially the notion that women maintain an unquestioning support for male decision-making. In both sections, women believed that in actively supporting the war, they should also have input into deciding how their support should be directed. In the process, both northern and southern women began to challenge male leaders and military policy. In the Confederacy, women in coastal communities like Charleston, Mobile, and Savannah began raising money specifically for the purchase of gunboats that could be used for "home defense." Their actions reflected an implicit rebuke to Confederate leaders who, they felt, were not doing enough to protect some of the more vulnerable southern ports. The confrontation between ladies' aid societies and Union leadership played out somewhat differently in the North, where, unlike the Confederacy, male leaders eventually took steps to centralize and bureaucratize the relief work under the rubric of the United States Sanitary Commission (USSC). But despite the USSC's organizational strengths, its leadership nonetheless encountered frequent and persistent challenges from local women who objected to Sanitary Commission procedures. More specifically, northern ladies' aid societies found themselves at loggerheads with USSC leadership when women insisted on sending supplies directly to soldiers and not to a central fund, to be disbursed as commission leaders saw fit. Worried that numbers of male commission leaders were mishandling their contributions, many northern women believed they could better determine and direct, on their own, how their donations should be used.[10]

Finally, in both sections, the energy and enthusiasm that women devoted to soldiers' relief work did not shield them against charges, especially later in the war, that they were, in fact, unpatriotic and unsupportive of their region's political objectives. At various points in the conflict, both Unionists and Confederates spoke out against what they perceived as a fading of feminine support. On the face of it, this should not be terribly surprising. For one, the zeal of the early war period did weaken and many women did withdraw, for a variety of reasons, from aid work. Moreover, as soldiers on both sides suffered military setbacks, and as both military and home-front morale declined, public commentators no doubt found it far less complicated to make women the scapegoats for that problem. If, as both northerners and southerners had argued, a successful military enterprise hinged on women's willingness to subordinate private claims to public demands, a floundering military enterprise could, conversely, be linked to women's unwillingness to make the necessary sacrifices. Many undoubtedly found it easier to blame selfish women for their nation's military woes than to blame military leaders or soldiers themselves. Women, after all, cast no votes for officials who might scold them, nor did they serve military leaders to whom they might become insubordinate. By February 1863, southern news articles faulted southern women for increasing desertion rates, a charge that would be echoed for the next two years. "Though the ladies may not be willing to concede the fact," said one North Carolina official late in the war, "they are nevertheless responsible . . . for the desertion in the army and the dissipation in the country." According to an 1864 correspondent to the *Montgomery Daily Advertiser*, Confederate women's "self-sacrifice has vanished; wives and maidens now labor only to exempt husbands and lovers from the perils of service."[11]

Not all women, of course, retreated from their Confederate sympathies. Virginia women may have been prodded by the constant and frequently obnoxious presence of Yankee soldiers to rekindle their ardor for the South. Others may have been motivated by youthful idealism or even personal feelings of love for a Confederate soldier to stay true to the southern cause. Yet considerable evidence has been presented that suggests growing numbers of Confederate women became less and less supportive of the South's military effort as Confederate defeat loomed larger on the wartime horizon. While it is questionable how much these women were the *source* of Confederate failure, their faltering patriotism was certainly a consequence of a collapsing military enterprise. And because the South had so carefully intertwined the cause of home with the cause of nation, suffering at home offered women, as well as men, a strong argument for abandoning their patriotism. "I cannot help being unpatriotic," said one older Virginia woman in the latter half of the war, "to feel a little selfish sometimes—and regret our peace and comfort in the old Union." When Yankee troops took control of most of her state, a Tennessee woman admitted to feeling "unpatriotic enough not to care a continental about it any way." Historian Drew Faust reads such remarks as indications of southern white women's new sense of self-interest, a determination to recognize, after four years of wartime suffering, their own needs as separate from those of their families and communities. To some extent, especially for elite white women, this is probably true. Yet I suspect that many southern white women renounced their patriotic support for the Confederate enterprise because they had lacked a strong foundation for endorsing the Confederate venture in the first place, because the ideology of the Confederacy had never really forced them to grapple with a political entity that stood outside their homes and families and immediate surroundings. For many southern women, home had been their paramount obligation at the war's outset, and it remained so at the war's conclusion.[12]

By 1863, Unionists were engaged in what may have been an even more heated debate on the patriotism of their womenfolk, dramatically reversing the enthusiastic tributes offered to the female sex when the conflict began. Indeed, nine months after offering initial praise for the "enthusiasm of the women," the New York *Herald* drew attention to the general problem of overindulgence among northerners, suggesting that, "in the case of the fair sex the extravagance is still greater." Women, they believed, would have to learn to divert their excessive clothing allowances into taxes that could be used "for the salvation of the Union." The *Herald* returned to this theme again in the fall of 1864. "In the South," they explained, "the ladies, who are by far more bitter secessionists than the men, have long since discarded the use of silks and satins. . . . With us the same sentiment has not as yet obtained." The widely published author Mary Abigail Dodge, who wrote under the pseudonym of Gail Hamilton, likewise took aim against northern civilians and women in particular. "The women of to-day," she wrote in the spring of 1863, "have not come up to the level of to-day. They do not stand abreast with its issues." But perhaps the most pointed barb came from the writer who believed that southern women had made the Confederate war effort strong while northern women had made the Union effort falter. "But for the courage and energy of the women of the South," this writer intoned, "we believe the Rebellion would not have survived to this time. Had the women of the North with like zeal addressed themselves to the work of encouraging a loyal and devoted spirit among us, the copperhead conspiracy in behalf of the enemy would have been strangled at its birth, and the rebels would have learned, long ago, the futility of expecting aid and comfort from such a source."[13]

Here, indeed, were sharp and bitter words, directed with increasing vehemence at those who, at least on the face of things, seemed to have little to do with how the war was being fought. Why did commentators feel the need to single out northern women for such abuse? Were women notably less supportive of the war than men, or did they, perhaps, have a distinctive responsibility in wartime which some felt they had neglected? And what did these attacks imply about the models northerners used to evaluate female patriotism? Although critics often spoke of northern women in bitter and unpleasant tones, their challenges—and especially the response those challenges generated—ultimately helped shift the terms by which northerners appraised women's national allegiance.

But before looking at how the standards shifted, I'd like to first suggest that the critique of northern women's patriotism was, in large part, not about women at all. Rather, the attack provided a way for northern writers and commentators to express concerns and anxieties about a number of other issues that they preferred not to address (or perhaps didn't know how to address) directly. Indeed, if war—as many scholars have observed—creates the perception of a strict gender division between a male battlefront and a female home front, then an attack on "woman" spoke to a broad range of domestic concerns that really involved the experiences and attitudes of both women and men but that perhaps assumed a particular resonance when presented specifically as women's failings.

One such issue was class. Certainly, as even a cursory glance at these critiques suggests, although writers aimed their barbs at "woman" in general, elite women were often the implicit villains in much of the literature. This spoke to a growing perception in the North that many inhabitants not only would escape the hardships of war but also might prosper and profit from the struggle. Many observers, both male and female, found it difficult to reconcile the comfort and prosperity in some quarters of the Union with the mounting death tolls and casualty lists from the battlefields. Gail Hamilton, for one, believed that the excessive amounts of material comforts that Unionists luxuriated in made them unworthy of military victory. Somehow, northerners should experience impoverishment, even if it was self-induced. Perhaps that, she believed, would spread the suffering equally across the class divide. Thus she urged her readers—and women in particular—to "take not acquiescently, but joyfully, the spoiling of your goods. Not only look poverty in the face with high disdain, but embrace it with gladness and welcome." The New York *Herald* likewise argued that women, more than men, suffered from the habit of excessive consumption and made its class critique even more obvious in singling out those ladies who had not yet given up their lace and diamonds for the cause. How, the argument seemed to go, could a people who still enjoyed luxuries and fine goods have really made the kinds of sacrifices that war required?[14]

Not that pundits neglected to criticize wealthy men, especially those who became government contractors and subcontractors and took advantage of wartime demands to pay workers indecently low wages while making excessive amounts of money from poorly manu-

In this October 1863 illustration, Harper's Weekly *called attention to the indulgent, and therefore disloyal, behavior of the wealthy contractor's wife, contrasted to the impoverished, and loyal, demeanor of the spouse of a Union soldier. (*Harper's Weekly, *October 24, 1863)*

factured goods. Yet females, I would argue, figured more prominently in these critiques because many saw women, by their very nature, as symbols for materialistic excess and luxurious indulgence. The fact that women played more significant roles as consumers than as producers and that their "work" in the domestic arena was generally assumed to be a far more leisurely enterprise than the "real" work undertaken by men made them easy targets for criticism. Among the sharpest critiques were those aimed at "Mrs. Shoddy," the fictionalized wife of a wealthy wartime manufacturer who, as the name implied, had grown rich from the production of inferior goods. In one *Harper's Weekly* story, for example, "Miss Clementia Shoddy" and her mother revealed their appalling lack of patriotism by "dancing and making merry, and throwing away fortunes on diamonds" while "our brothers and sons are dying on battle-fields." In similar fashion, a *Harper's* illustration from October 1863 offered a series of scenes depicting "service and shoddy" in which the most

The Problem of Women's Patriotism 49

prominent figures were not the soldier, nor even the wartime contractor, but "the soldier's wife" and "the contractor's wife," the latter dressed extravagantly in silk while on a shopping trip for yet more stuff. In this representation the greedy, high-spending woman provided the ultimate symbol of wartime disloyalty.[15]

In fact, this pairing of the soldier's wife and the contractor's wife hints at where the really pressing class anxieties lay. To some extent, I think, the rhetoric that lashed out at the "Misses Shoddies" was offered as an appeal to the poorer women and men, the struggling soldiers and soldiers' wives (or potential soldiers and soldiers' wives), whose own patriotism was wavering after Union setbacks in 1862 and whose commitment to the Union cause—given the numbers of potential recruits in their ranks—was critical to Union success. In this way, observers may have hoped to rally the patriotism of working-class northerners by presenting their sacrifices as nobler and more meaningful, precisely because they cut so deep. The writer Fanny Fern, for example, heaped praise on all the soldiers' wives in an 1862 article in the New York *Ledger*; but she singled out for special praise "the wife of the poor soldier, who in giving her husband to her country has given everything." By suggesting that the ranks of the disloyal consisted largely of the rich, and of rich women in particular, prowar pundits may have hoped to stimulate northern working-class support for the war effort. The enemy to be rallied against, they implied, was not just the aristocratic slaveowner of the South but also the affluent and selfish lady of the North.[16]

The critique of northern women's patriotism also reflected Union anxiety, especially by the second and third years of the war, about the increasingly vocal antiwar politics of the Democratic Party. Women, so the commentators claimed, stood at the forefront of the so-called copperhead conspiracy, spearheading the position that urged a negotiated settlement with the South and a hasty conclusion to the war. But did women, especially nineteenth-century women, who were basically considered political nonentities, really have that much political clout? Certainly great numbers of women belonged to families that favored Democratic policies and Democratic candidates, including the emerging peace Democratic, or copperhead, position of the later war years. There is also evidence of women becoming more public in expressing pro-Democratic sympathies, particularly when pro-Democratic meant expressing opposition to the war. As the conflict persisted and the possibility of a Union victory seemed remote, Union officials, often with a good deal of justification, worried that women might feel the pull of the Democratic position and discourage their male kin from serving. A Republican official in New Hampshire urged the celebrated lecturer Anna Dickinson to make a special trip to his state in order to speak specifically to "the women in this state who have sons in the war" and "want the war closed." His plea came in February 1863, certainly a low point for the Union military effort. Late in the war, the Democratic position continued to have considerable pull on women's sentiments. Ann Cotton observed a rally in her Ohio village in October 1864 for Clement Vallandigham, one of the most notorious copperhead politicians. "Women and children helped form the procession," she wrote in a letter to her husband, "that marched him through town." In some places, like Ohio, Indiana, and Illinois, where support for antiwar Democrats was high, there may have even been a tendency for women to assume a greater burden in articulating the Democratic position because men feared being targeted as traitors or draft resisters. When Iowan Marjorie Rogers canvassed her rural community to get aid for soldiers, she found that she was "oftener insulted by women than men" because the men there had been warned by the county's Democratic sheriff to keep a low profile.[17]

The institution of the draft stirred up intense opposition to the Lincoln administration, on women's part, and in favor of the Democrats. "I am a copperhead and I can fight too," declared one angry female protester to a group of black women during the New York City draft riot. In Ohio, in October 1864, Jane Evans decried the draft for the suffering it would cause to "mamas and children" and insisted to her cousin Sam, a soldier in the Union army, that, despite his irritation with her antiwar position, she would "never change my politics as long as I live." Her declaration signaled that she would always be a Democrat, unlike Sam, who had shifted his partisan affiliation to the Republicans. It may be, too, that women's presence in antiwar activity, regardless of their numerical significance, received extra attention in journalists' accounts, because their involvement in any kind of political event was so unusual. Although scholarly accounts argue that women made up a minority of the protesters, news reports detailing the New York City draft riot often gave women a prominent place in the ranks of the rioters. "A large number of workingmen's wives," one New York *Herald* account explained, "began also to assemble along the various avenues, and, if anything, were more excited than the men."[18]

The notion of excitable working-class women rioting against the draft, regardless of how many women actually did count themselves in the ranks of Democracy's supporters, provided the Republican press with an important political symbol. Specifically, those irate women represented the unmanliness of the antiwar, Democratic viewpoint. In this way, the chastisement of northern women for a lack of patriotism reflected, among other things, a partisan attack on Democratic men. What, after all, did it say about men if their political sympathies followed the lead of treacherous and untrustworthy women whose actions were devoid of reasoned political thinking? The very fact that women had inserted themselves so prominently into this political discussion—not in a demure, behind-the-scenes way like those who encouraged men to serve—could be read as an indication that the Democratic position was not to be trusted. This was the message conveyed, at least in part, by the 1862 political cartoon "Candidates for the Exempt Brigade" in which one of the so-called candidates is an angry-looking female who has made it possible for her male relative to be excused from military action by doing the cold-hearted work of chopping off his finger. Although the cartoon's central figure is the draft-dodging man, he stands between those who seem to have even more suspect motivations: the conniving politician who will provide the exemption and the manipulative woman who has incapacitated her relative for military service.

CANDIDATES FOR THE EXEMPT BRIGADE.—

*In this 1862 political cartoon, a sour-faced woman helps a man avoid serving
in the Union army when she cuts off his finger. (Library of Congress,
Prints and Photographs Division)*

But if class and political considerations shaped some of the discussion of northern women's disloyalty, the literature also introduced a comparative perspective for considering this female betrayal of the Union cause. As the editorials and magazine articles implied, northern women failed where southern women had not. Southern women had sacrificed, but northern women seemed relatively untouched by sacrifice; female Confederates had shown "courage" and "energy" and proved themselves "bitter secessionists," but northern women lacked "zeal" and failed to "come up to the level of to-day." If northern women, then, found the challenges of patriotism beyond them, why was the same not true for the women of the Confederacy? The comparisons suggested some of the problems inherent in evaluating patriotism more generally and the specific problem in evaluating women's patriotism on the Union side. Unlike the women of the revolutionary period, or of the Confederacy, northern women (with

The Problem of Women's Patriotism 53

the exception of some in Pennsylvania and in the border states) weren't being asked to open their homes to soldiers on the march or to men wounded after a battle. Rather, they were being asked to demonstrate the right kind of "spirit" or display their enthusiastic "zeal." In this regard, some of the criticism of northern women's patriotism stemmed from the fact that northern women were being asked to rally around something that women usually didn't rally around: not just their men, or their homes, or their "homeland," but a nation-state and its corresponding political and ideological rationale.

Indeed, the attack on female Unionists' loyalty was not unlike the concern expressed about Union soldiers and how they would sustain their commitment to "matters abstract and intangible." When, in their private correspondence, Union soldiers compared themselves to Confederate soldiers, they sounded sometimes like those public commentators who compared women in the North to their counterparts in the South. Some men suggested that their own fighting spirit was not as animated because they weren't struggling for the material things—like homes and families—the way rebel soldiers were. Confederates, an Illinois sergeant believed, "fought like Devils" because they battled to "protect [their] property." Moreover, if the Union goals seemed remote and intangible for Union soldiers, certainly they would have seemed exceptionally abstract, and therefore perhaps less inspiring, for northern women. In a certain way, then, the northern public was debating the question of just what female patriotism should consist of: unswerving support of men and their cause, or commitment to the broader principles of the nation and its government? And, if the latter, would women really be able to muster that kind of commitment to something that stood so clearly outside their sphere?[19]

Northern women had no intention of letting the charges against them go unanswered. Unlike Confederate women, many of whom acknowledged that their loyalty to country was naturally faltering in the face of domestic suffering, Union women often took pains to rebut the charges of disloyalty and to demonstrate more decisively their commitment to the Union cause. Some mounted a very traditional defense of female patriotism, arguing that women were prepared to do the time-honored work of supporting whatever position their men adopted, and would do so in quiet and unassuming ways. But some women challenged these conventional attitudes and embraced a new view that held women individually responsible for their own political positions.

On the traditional side was a response that brought women back to one of the most conventional acts of female patriotism: the consumer boycott. In May of 1864, a group of women gathered in Washington, DC, and formed an association they called "The Ladies' National Covenant." Initiated by a number of women who traveled in elite Washington circles, including the widow of Stephen Douglas and the wives of senators and military officers, the Ladies' National Covenant aimed to rebut the charges of northern women's luxurious (and unpatriotic) indulgences by pledging "for three years, or for the war . . . to each other and the country to purchase no imported article of apparel." A somewhat questionable economic rationale stood behind the pledge. "The gold that goes from the country [to buy imported fabrics]," the society's organizers explained, "detracts from the pay of the soldier who is fighting for our salvation, and diminishes the wages of our sister women, who toil for their bread, into a miserable pittance that scarcely suffices to keep them from starvation." Women who worked in the domestic textile industries may have benefited from a concerted effort to boost the sales of home manufacture, but it also seems likely that most of the increased profit would have found its way into the pockets of their employers. And how, precisely, this movement to buy domestic fabrics would have enhanced the soldier's paycheck remained unclear. Mary Lincoln, in fact, opposed the movement because it would result—given the loss of tariff proceeds—in decreased federal revenue. Indeed the shakiness of the economic rationale suggested that the Ladies' National Covenant formed not so much to address a compelling economic dilemma but because elite women felt obligated to show their patriotism.[20]

Toward this end, the Ladies' National Covenant turned back in time for their model of female patriotism. "In 1770 the women of Massachusetts, actuated by the same impulse that inspires us, assembled in the city of Boston" where they "signed a pledge to abstain from the use of tea, the greatest luxury of the time." Eventually, these women of old refused to purchase a wide array of imported goods, and thus "the flax-wheel, the hatchet, and the hand-loom became sublime instruments of freedom in the hands of American women." Perhaps not surprisingly, the covenant's organizers made reference only to New England women, conveniently ignoring the southern women who participated prominently in the revolutionary-era boycotts. Still, the real point, as the Ladies' National Covenant saw it, was that these women demonstrated their patriotism by domestic sacrifice, by enduring hardship and deprivation in the service of their cause. Thus the ladies of the covenant did not directly dispute the argument depicting northern women as more dedicated purchasers than patriots. Rather, they acknowledged the problem of excessive spending—that there were, indeed, too many "Misses Shoddies" in their midst—and aimed to demonstrate their patriotism by becoming less excessive. In this, they adhered to the model of female patriotism that they saw operating at the time of the Revolution and, more importantly, in the Civil War South. Let the spirit of frugality and sacrifice "animate the women of the North as it does the women of the South, to their credit be it spoken," wrote one supporter of the pledge, "and our brave soldiers in the field will feel more like fighting, and will fight with more ardor."[21]

Yet, ultimately, the covenant enjoyed little success or widespread support. It suffered, in part, from having formed around a plan that was largely irrelevant to the patriotic demands placed before Union women. True, there might have been something symbolic in dressing plainly and simply while the war was in progress, but the kind of boycott that was urged could never have had the political effect that it had in the American colonies or in the Confederate South, where boycotts represented a political statement on behalf of one's cause and in direct opposition to the enemy's financial well-being. Likewise, a campaign to forego expensive foreign fabrics held little meaning for the majority of northern women who didn't buy those things in the first place. "When they get down to bread and water," remarked the exceedingly unostentatious Clara Barton, "I will listen to them." Ultimately, what the Ladies' National Covenant failed to see was how the nature of the Union struggle was pushing women toward a different type of political expression, one that could not be articulated in ways traditionally associated with female patriotism.[22]

Pushing at the boundaries of tradition were those women who had begun to recognize how the Union struggle was prompting women to make an independent expression of their own political viewpoint. Just as the separation of national and domestic causes forced many Union men to give greater emphasis to ideological and political motivations than Confederates did, so did some northern women likewise embrace the need to support the more abstract cause of nation over the more pressing concerns of home. As some women reasoned, if they consented to their loved ones' service, they also consented to a cause that made certain political and ideological principles more important than the defense of home and family. They said, in effect, "I agree that in this struggle the nation ranks higher than home and so I, too, will support the nation." "I expect I feel only as every true American woman feels," explained Eliza Otis in a letter to one of her husband's comrades, "that all who have taken up arms in this hour of our Country's need and peril, who taking their lives in their hands have gone forth to strike for the defence of Freedom and all the sacred rights of man, have a claim upon our sympathies, and should be loved and cherished by every loyal heart in the land." Sophia Buchanan, whose husband fought with a Michigan regiment, also embraced the national cause, despite the misgivings she felt about her husband's absence. The conflict, she explained, was "no slight struggle, [but] a matter of life & death, to the most glorious nation, the sun ever shone upon."[23]

Few spoke this language more forcefully than African American women, especially the free black women of the North. Although initially denied the possibility of laying claim to a national cause, black men and women gradually came to embrace the Union struggle, even to the point of expressing some degree of patriotic attachment to U.S. institutions and symbols, as that struggle increasingly entwined itself with the cause of slave liberation. Thus freedom—which included the freedom to create and maintain autonomous homes and families—offered a route by which African Americans came to elevate the importance of the national struggle, sometimes even above homes and families. Among free black women, especially in the North, this encouraged enthusiastic expressions of Union loyalty, although loyalty that—as many explained—hinged on the commitment to emancipation. "Just a little while since," explained black abolitionist Frances Ellen Harper during the Civil War, "the American flag to the flying bondman was an ensign of bondage, now it has become a symbol of protection and freedom." The ex-slave Sojourner Truth likewise embraced the flag and the flag's representatives for similar reasons. Called upon to defend the Republican Party against Indiana copperheads, Truth did so with gusto, beginning one speaking appearance by joining in as the audience sang the "Star Spangled Banner." "I sang," she recalled, "with all my might."[24]

But before we accept such expressiveness as a new form of female patriotism, we need to investigate just what these words and ideas meant to the women who spoke them—or sang them. Had these women simply done what women, traditionally, were expected to do: to accept and endorse the political beliefs that their husbands and male kin upheld? Undoubtedly, in some cases, yes. But I would argue that Union women, both black and white, increasingly did something else: they began to hold themselves to a new standard of patriotism, grappling with the ideological and political content of their patriotism and making their political and ideological utterances their own, through their words and their actions and through a new level of political accountability. Black women, in particular, especially those who had been enslaved, probably already had a tradition of independent political expression, borne of the general disregard shown to the black family and to black men's political standing. In the course of the war, northern white women also began to recognize that there was more to patriotism than simply assenting to the demands of men.

Such was the contention advanced by the anonymous author who penned "A Few Words in Behalf of the Loyal Women of the United States by One of Themselves," an 1863 pamphlet issued by the Loyal Publication Society, a propaganda wing of the Union cause. Carefully investigating the differences between Union and Confederate women's patriotism, the author observed how southern women were often praised for enduring home-front suffering; but northern women, she noted, could not be expected to endure the same type of deprivation. "It is no virtue," she observed with respect to southern ladies' suffering, "to wear a coarse dress if you can obtain no other." Perhaps of even greater importance, the writer argued, was that northern women displayed their patriotism differently from Confederate women, the former having feelings that were "deep" rather than "violent" and a "quiet and constant" sense of duty "rather than a headlong or impetuous impulse." Some of this reflected the author's intent to defend northern women for possessing a more refined, and even traditionally feminine, sense of modesty compared to the loud and demonstrative females of the South. But beyond this, she was also trying to come to terms with the essential problem of Union women's patriotism, that is, their attempt to grapple with the broader, intellectual, and abstract problems of the conflict, the fact that they were not, in most cases, defending something concrete and tangible. "Never," she urged her female readers, "be persuaded to regret that you have not stimulated the angry passions of your countrymen, whose high and holy cause is incitement enough for all brave and true hearts." In other words, her argument went, Union women had distinguished themselves because they were committed to a principle of liberty, a principle that ranked higher than anything that animated the men and women of the South.[25]

The essential difficulty with Confederate women's patriotism, the writer suggested, turned out to be precisely the thing that was supposed to define female patriotism in the first place: they had given their unswerving support to men. To develop this position, the author assumed that southern white women did not, in fact, have the same interest as men in perpetuating slavery, that they had, at times, expressed opposition to the institution, but had now, regrettably, chosen to blindly follow their men in supporting a war in its defense. Thus these women could not be excused for doing what women "usually" do in accepting "the political views of the husbands," but must be held accountable for doing "everything possible to incite and encourage" their men in their "determination to found an empire whose corner-stone should be human slavery." It was time, in other words, to acknowledge the fact that Confederate women's so-called patriotism reflected not "a sacrifice in the cause of truth" but a commitment to the goal of treason.[26]

Other northern women elaborated on themes introduced by the author of "A Few Words in Behalf of the Loyal Women." More specifically, they rejected the notion of female political innocence that allowed Confederate women, or even northern women who leaned toward the Democrats, to hide behind a banner of neutral, and politically disinterested, patriotism, failing to take responsibility for the positions they espoused. If women, they argued, acted like traitors, they should be treated as such. "I have heard," wrote New Yorker Ruth Whittemore to her soldier brother, "that ladies down [South] will spit at our soldiers and if one ever spits at you I want you to slap her ears soundly." Others went beyond the notion of confronting individual rebel women for their rude behavior and argued that, as a whole, Confederate women bore a tremendous onus for the war and must be held responsible. "O these guilty, guilty women," proclaimed the Michigan journalist Lois Adams upon the war's conclusion. "They have a fearful responsibility for the aid they have given in plotting, planning and pushing on the rebellion."[27]

Even more important when it came to establishing a new standard for female patriotism was the fact that most Union military officials ultimately agreed with Lois Adams. They enacted her idea—of holding women responsible for their individual beliefs and actions—in their implementation of wartime loyalty oaths. By the end of 1862, as the Union army pursued a more aggressive war of occupation in

the South, many Union commanders began relying on a more extensive system of oath-taking. Requiring southern civilians to swear
their past and future loyalty to the U.S. government, Union officers used the so-called ironclad oath system to gain a more stable
foothold in sections of the Confederacy. And, since southern white
women had by now gained a widespread reputation as fervent upholders of the Confederate cause, the argument that they might be
exempt from oath-taking, on account of their sex, was increasingly
losing ground.

Traditional notions of female patriotism rested on the assumption
that women showed their loyalty simply by endorsing their men's
beliefs. In contrast, the new policies of the Civil War era suggested
that women would have to take responsibility for those beliefs and
that usual assumptions about women's patriotism could not be used
as a pretext to let southern women off the hook. "It is absolutely
essential to the entire security of the commands in this vicinity,"
explained the Union commander near Fairfax Court House, Virginia, in March of 1863, "that the women and other irresponsible
persons in this neighborhood be compelled to take the oath, or [be]
placed outside the lines." The emphatic language suggested that this
was, indeed, a new way of thinking about women's loyalty (or disloyalty), one that might not have been consistent with traditional
ways of waging war. Nonetheless, what seemed to be emerging was a
view that insisted on making southern white women more accountable for their anti-Union sentiments, and to have them take personal
responsibility for their "irresponsible" views. No doubt this was a
position that was hard, even for some Unionists, to adopt; hence the
need for frequent and strong reminders about this policy from the
Union high command. In 1865 the Massachusetts-born sculptor John
Rogers offered his rendition of the Civil War's new political imperative in his widely popular statue, "Taking the Oath." In Rogers's
sculpture, the somewhat hesitant and uncertain Union soldier—
should he remove his hat in the presence of a lady?—knows he must
ask even a woman in the South to take an oath of loyalty if she wishes
to receive food, but he appears slightly awkward about doing so.

TAKING THE OATH
DRAWING AND RATIONS

Photographed and Engraved by Penfield. From a Statuette by John Rogers.

This Harper's Weekly *engraving from 1866 depicts John Rogers's statue, "Taking the Oath and Drawing Rations," in which an elite southern woman is shown taking an oath of loyalty to the United States so that she may receive food. Rogers's depiction suggests some confusion on the Union officer's part, now required to ensure that even women make a pledge of national allegiance. The young African American boy who looks on—no doubt a former slave—seems also to register some confusion about the changed relations of power. (*Harper's Weekly, July 21, 1866*)

Observing the scene is an African American boy, no doubt a newly freed slave, who seems intrigued by the new form of obedience the war has generated when even ex-slave mistresses must comply with federal authorities. Rogers's statue was, apparently, ambiguous enough in its political sympathies to appeal to both northern and southern audiences. Southerners may well have read Rogers's work as an accurate rendering of southern white women's deplorable humiliation, while northerners may have read it simply as a reflection of the revolutionary changes, however one might feel about them, wrought by war. In any event, Rogers captured one of the indelible alterations the war introduced: women's new political accountability to the Union military.[28]

The policy of holding southern women accountable to their political beliefs continued into the postwar period. Now women might be required to take loyalty oaths in order to get certain jobs or to reclaim confiscated property. Thus while the Massachusetts court had argued, after the American Revolution, that "a feme-covert was never holden to take an oath of allegiance" because married women had no political identity distinct from their husbands, Reconstruction policy routinely demanded that southern white women take their places in the new social order by demonstrating their personal loyalty. The Southern Claims Commission, the government body that officiated on southerners' claims to confiscated property, insisted that women, just like men, demonstrate their loyalty to the U.S. government before they could possess land or crops seized during the war. Indeed, even if she were the rightful heir of a man of proven loyalty, a woman would have to make an independent demonstration of her own allegiance before her property rights would be recognized.[29]

IN THE SPRING OF 1863 a group of female activists approached the problem of women's patriotism not from the negative perspective of Confederate women's treason but from the positive perspective of encouraging and nurturing the loyalty of women in the North. Spurred by the creation of all-male loyal leagues among Union supporters, Susan B. Anthony and Elizabeth Cady Stanton led the efforts to organize the Woman's Loyal National League in May 1863. Like the author of "A Few Words in Behalf of the Loyal Women," Stanton and Anthony sought to counter the charge of disloyalty with a new evaluation of female patriotism, patriotism that had less to do with women's unwavering support for men and more to do with understanding and upholding political principles. Putting aside prewar calls for women's rights and women's suffrage, Stanton and Anthony turned their efforts toward giving women a political voice in the Union struggle. "We have heard many complaints," wrote Stanton in the original "call" for the organization, "of the lack of enthusiasm among Northern women; but when a mother lays her son on the altar of her country, she asks an object equal to the sacrifice." The point, in other words, was not simply for women to make patriotic sacrifices on behalf of their country but for women to have a full appreciation and understanding of the goals and principles for which "their country" stood. "If it can be true that loyal women are lukewarm," Susan B. Anthony echoed in her own remarks at the gathering, "it is because the objects of the war have been confused." Thus one critical objective of Stanton and Anthony's wartime organizing was to assert northern women's patriotism by providing a clear political and ideological basis—specifically in the struggle to defeat slavery—for female loyalty. Ernestine Rose further expanded upon this idea in arguing that she was not "unconditionally loyal" but was "loyal to one thing, and that was freedom and humanity." Yet another representative of the Loyal League argued on behalf of fostering "a healthy, intelligent patriotism in the social and domestic circles of our land," one that rested not only on supporting the men who served but also on cultivating "a true understanding and appreciation of the principles of our democratic institutions."[30]

Such arguments further encouraged northerners to see women in a more explicitly political and even partisan light. Indeed, Stanton and Anthony hoped to insert themselves, and women's voices more generally, into shaping Republican policy and getting the party to take a more radical position on emancipation. Others likewise recognized that women's patriotism might well require them to demonstrate their Republican political sympathies more explicitly. If, as critics had suggested, northern women's lukewarm patriotism had created a more hospitable climate for copperhead politics, then, as some respondents argued, women must be acknowledged as individuals who possessed a distinctive political voice, a voice that could be just as loud in denouncing Democrats as in supporting them. Robert Hubbard, a surgeon with the Seventeenth Connecticut Volunteer Regiment, urged his wife to discard outmoded notions about female reticence and vociferously declare her political allegiances: "I know ladies are not usually interested in such matters, but the time has come when they as well as the sterner sex must put a shoulder to the wheel." Apparently putting a shoulder to the wheel entailed, for Hubbard, "spit[ting] upon those who manifest" Democratic leanings. Taylor Peirce likewise wished to see his own wife take on a more active role in making her patriotic politics manifest. Hoping to see the commander of his regiment defeat the copperhead candidate for the Iowa governor's seat, Peirce urged his wife "to do all you can for him to get him in there." Increasingly, it seems, northerners had begun to concede that politics was very much women's business. With so many men absent from their local communities, women became more visible in local politics, if not as candidates and voters then certainly as observers and discussants. Women, in other words, had a special responsibility to speak up more strongly for a Republican position because so many Republican men were away at war.[31]

This, I would add, reflected a uniquely northern set of circumstances. With Confederate politics dominated by a one-party system, partisanship tended to be muted for all Confederates, men as well as women. Southern women thus might express apathy or disgust, or even support, with the Confederate government, but they generally did not channel those views through the vehicle of a political party. This is not to deny political divisions within the Confederacy, including the bitter factions that formed against and in support of Jefferson Davis, but the lack of formal party organizing meant that Confederate women could never avail themselves of the same kind of political education—in terms of party organizing and campaigning—that was available to northern women. As a result, southern women remained, and would continue to remain after the war, marginal to nineteenth-century American political culture's most important institution.

For northern women, in contrast, the Civil War tended to heighten their sense of partisanship and thus helped draw them more closely into the nation's political life. And while women certainly affiliated with both parties, I suspect that the Republicans, who were generally less insistent than the Democrats on a hypermasculine culture of campaigning and electioneering, provided a more hospitable home for women. Indeed, in what may have been perhaps the ultimate acknowledgment of women's political influence, the Republican leadership hired a woman—the youthful and energetic Anna Dickinson—as a campaign stump speaker and encouraged her to sway women, as well as men, back into the Republican camp. By early 1863 Dickinson had emerged as a prominent Republican lecturer, taking her message to audiences throughout New England and later to Pennsylvania. Less famous women also took the opportunity, especially as the partisan scene became more heated in the midwar period, to express their pro-Republican sympathies. As the 1864 presidential campaign moved into gear, Emeline Ritner found that politics influenced her personal connections. "When I know a person is 'copperhead,'" she explained to her husband, "I *can't* feel that they are *my* friends." After local Democratic victories in her upstate New York community in 1863, Ruth Whittemore put her Republican politics even more openly on the line. Outraged at the men in her town whose treasonous views were "upheld by the democratic party while it pretends to be loyal," Whittemore responded to one Democratic supporter who questioned the justness of the war. "I told him," she explained to her brother in the army, "I thought men never fought in a better or a more just cause than ours."[32]

IN THE COURSE OF THE DEBATE on northern women's patriotism, old assumptions about female loyalty gradually began to disintegrate. If, as critics maintained, northern women lacked the patriotic fervor

Anna Dickinson became famous for her youthful, fiery oratory, evidenced in the many lectures she delivered, some under the official sponsorship of the Republican Party, during the Civil War. (Library of Congress, Prints and Photographs Division)

of their southern sisters, then the respondents replied that Unionists had erred in simply assuming that women would adopt the traditionally patriotic pose of endorsing whatever their menfolk believed. Instead, as Anna Dickinson's lecture tour and as Stanton and Anthony's organizing efforts suggested, women had to ground their patriotism in their own individual understandings of the Union cause. For some this meant a more explicit endorsement of the Republican Party; for others it meant dedicating themselves more forcefully to the cause of emancipation. Moreover, as the war progressed, it became increasingly apparent to many that "loyalty" and "patriotism" could not be used as screens behind which pro-Confederate women might hide. Rather, their patriotism, too, had to be judged in terms of political beliefs to which they would be held individually accountable. As I consider in the next—and last—chapter, northern women drew on the wartime notion of individual political accountability in the way they chose to honor the memory of northern women during the Civil War. Yet, in doing so, they also ultimately directed Union women away from creating an enduring memory of their Civil War experience. It was, in contrast, the memory of Confederate women and their experiences that came, increasingly, to dominate the public imagination in the postwar era.

Union and Confederate Women and the Memory of the Civil War

IF ANYTHING UNITED THE divided sections at the time of the Civil War, it may have been the way gender so powerfully shaped the ideas—and the wartime activities—of male and female participants. Yet, as we've seen, gender also pushed northerners and southerners in very different directions. Confederate ideology, in reflecting white southern men's desire to sustain a patriarchal system that made them masters over slaves as well as white family members, emphasized a melding of home and country in the fight against the Union. In this way, the Confederate cause elevated white women as principal objects of obligation and thus encouraged those women to see themselves as vital components of the southern struggle, the essential foundation, in effect, for which that cause had been launched. But despite the spotlight cast on white womanhood, Confederate ideology did little to give women themselves an investment in any kind of national enterprise, or even in their region's political culture. The Confederacy did little to advance the civic identity of southern white women because the Confederate nation, by most accounts, could never really demand greater allegiance and fidelity—from either men or women—than the very localized attachments to home and hearth. Even more, the political atmosphere of the Confederate South, particularly the absence of active partisanship, had the effect of further stifling southern white women's political imaginations.

Northern women, in contrast, never figured as prominently as objects of obligation in the articulation of the Union cause. Mothers, it seems, tended to come in a distant third—outranked by God and country—when Union soldiers prioritized their commitments. Yet Union women did increasingly feel a sense of investment in a national enterprise and, to a growing extent, began to articulate their own political and ideological beliefs that demonstrated that investment. This, I believe, gave greater substance to the response northern women offered to the midwar attack on their patriotism, allowing them a chance to present themselves as defenders not just of homes and families but of a national cause, of an ideological principle, and, sometimes, of a political party. Increasingly, northern women and men distanced themselves from a long-standing view of female loyalty, one that assumed that women would simply follow their men's positions in wartime. Instead, as loyalty oaths and land confiscation policies suggested, Union administrators fully intended to hold women accountable for the views they expressed.

Many of these differences—in terms of how prominently women figured as objects of obligation and how women began to define their civic allegiance—carried over into the postwar period. They can be seen, most strikingly, in the very different and distinctive traditions of Civil War remembrance: how northern and southern women participated in postwar memorial activities and how much they did, or did not, themselves become the objects of postwar remembering. Indeed, to look back on the Civil War from the standpoint of the mid-twentieth century and to survey the monuments that had been built and the tributes that had been written, an observer might imagine that no group was more vital to the struggle than the white women of the South and no group more inconsequential than the women who supported the Union. In popular magazines devoted to wartime reminiscing, northern women were strikingly absent. In postwar fiction and cinema, Scarlett O'Hara and Melanie Wilkes overwhelmed whatever fleeting appearances Union women made on screen or stage. For every three Confederate soldiers' monuments that included tributes to women, only one Union monument did the same. And a Washington, DC, memorial originally conceived as a homage to Union women ended up focusing greater attention and publicity on the white women of the South. In this final chapter, I consider just how and why we have been left with these sharply contrasting legacies of northern and southern women in the Civil War.[1]

Southern white women became—early on in the postwar period—prominent participants in Confederate memorialization. By the spring of 1866, dozens of ladies memorial associations could ·be found in towns and cities throughout the South. At the most basic level, such organizations helped communities deal with the grief that accompanied the Confederacy's staggering death rate. With an estimated 260,000 military deaths and perhaps another 50,000 civilian deaths, postwar southerners inhabited a world in which one-quarter of southern white men of military age had died. Because men constituted the overwhelming majority of the dead, perhaps, then, it was fitting, even necessary, for women to come forward in the memorial work. Foremost in those efforts were the wives of many prominent southern leaders and former Confederate officers who joined organizations dedicated to overseeing the burying and reburying of Confederate soldiers. Women in these memorial societies supervised the construction of cemeteries, moved the dead from one location to another, raised funds for monuments, and arranged for Memorial Day ceremonies. In subsequent decades, southern white women would remain highly visible in the commemorative movement, although their work had less to do with the gritty work of reburial and more with the celebratory work of remembrance. By the 1890s, southern white women had assumed primary responsibility for the construction of numerous Confederate monuments and memorials, and were encouraging the writing and publication of historical works that sympathetically portrayed the South's Civil War experience. With the formation of the United Daughters of the Confederacy (UDC) in 1894, southern white women would solidify their hold on Confederate remembering and would continue to make a significant mark on the memorial landscape.[2]

To a great extent, southern women's prominence in this work was shaped by the particular conditions of defeat and occupation that prevailed in the postwar South. In this respect, it certainly made a difference that southern women lived in the place where the most soldiers had died. The Confederate dead sometimes literally rested on the doorsteps of southern women, making the problem of burying and memorializing those dead something immediate, pressing, and local. True, there were some long-distance efforts involved, including moving dead Confederates from places like Gettysburg back to southern graveyards. But, by and large, southern women often acted out of a strong, localized impulse: to tend to the graves of those who had died in their communities, including soldiers who may have been cared for by local women. Obviously, in the North, there was not the same local imperative. Tending to the Union dead—at least those whose bodies remained on southern soil—required a different type of geographical orientation, not to mention physical capabilities, which simply from a practical standpoint would have been hard for women to adopt. The Ladies Memorial Association of Columbus, Georgia, though, did not face those kinds of obstacles: their organization evolved out of the Soldier's Aid Society that local women had formed during the war to tend to sick and wounded soldiers in the nearby hospital. Shifting their focus shortly after the war ended, these women now directed their work to caring for the graves of the Confederate dead (which included many former hospital patients) in their local cemetery.[3]

Southern white women did for Confederate soldiers what the federal government was doing, throughout the country, on behalf of Union soldiers. In this regard, the women of the former Confederacy stepped in to fill a vacuum that, in the North, was occupied by government officials. Union soldiers who fell on southern, as well as northern, battlefields came under the jurisdiction of the U.S. War Department and so beyond the purview of northern women. Even during the war, the roots were laid for a national cemetery system by which the federal government would exercise ultimate authority in creating and maintaining cemeteries throughout the United States where the final remains of the Union dead would rest. Certainly, in many places, civilians participated in the commemorative work. Yet, even still, federal and state governments played a dominant role in funding the construction of cemeteries and dispatching agents to assist with the identification and reburial of bodies. Such efforts, at least to some extent, preempted northern women from Union memorializing efforts. But because federal officials and directives largely ignored the Confederate dead, a door was opened for southern white women to make this cause their own. "Legislative enactment may not be made to do honor to" the memories of fallen Confederates, intoned the secretary of the Columbus, Georgia, Ladies Memorial Association. But the ladies, she believed, "can keep alive the memory of the debt we owe them."[4]

Indeed, the very hostility of the federal government to Confederate commemoration may have also helped create the conditions that allowed women to play such a prominent part in this movement. In his study of southern memory and postwar politics, William Blair observes that white women and men may have recognized a political, as well as practical, expedient in allowing the women to take the helm. Put simply, women could become the public face of the Confederacy and its cause in a period when federal occupation made it more difficult for southern white men to preach anything that smacked of sectionalism. A Georgia newspaper recalled that women actively took up memorial work for the Confederacy because the men "were under parole and were pledged not to aid or encourage any movement of that kind." Worried that the burial of the Confederate dead could become an occasion for anti-Reconstruction politics, federal officials sometimes intervened in and clamped down on southern commemorative efforts. But, according to the ex-Confederates, it would be absurd to read sinister political motivations into the loving and sentimental tributes of women. "Political significance is not attached to these funeral ceremonies in the South," argued a columnist for the *Richmond Whig*. "They are conducted by the ladies, and it is not the habit of the Southern ladies to form political conspiracies."[5]

Which is not to say, of course, that there was no political content to these female-run events. William Blair notes that women frequently chose Decoration Day speakers who had pointedly sectional, and clearly anti-Republican, agendas. But those events—and those speakers—could operate under the cloak of feminine sentiment and thus, to some extent, below the radar of federal officials. Again we have the words of the Columbus Ladies Memorial Association: The worst radical, explained the society's secretary, "could not refuse us the simple privilege of paying honor to those who died defending the life, honor and happiness of the Southern women."[6]

Here in this quote we can glimpse yet another reason why southern white women became so central to Confederate commemoration. To repeat one of the themes suggested previously: During the war—and in ways that differed significantly from Unionist pronouncements—Confederate ideology had made the defense of hearth and home central to the southern struggle and, as such, had placed southern white women at the heart of the Confederate imagination. As a result, when the secretary of the Columbus organization spoke of honoring those who "died defending the life, honor and happiness of the Southern women," she spoke words that were not simply created to serve some postwar mythology. Rather, her language reflected precisely the wartime calculation that so many Confederate soldiers made: that they fought to protect homes and families from the "black" Republicans of the North whose views and policies threatened to destroy the domestic foundation of southern society and southern slavery. And here, I think, we begin to get some clue not only why southern white women became important actors in the postwar commemoration process but also why those women figured so prominently as symbols in Confederate memory. The Lost Cause ideology—the confluence of ideas and images by which white southerners remembered the causes and outcomes of the Civil War—drew significantly on the Confederates' wartime agenda that had repeatedly placed women and families central to the Confederate cause. In this regard, the Lost Cause movement sought to recapture the patriarchal world of the old South by symbolically employing white women as the central worshippers of male Confederate veterans. The central placement of southern white women gave force and vitality to the conservative political and social agenda of the Lost Cause. And like the Confederate agenda itself, the Lost Cause obscured its politics by bringing seemingly neutral domestic goals, and ethereal white women, to the fore.[7]

As southerners, over time, constructed a rationale for secession and the war's objectives, they fashioned a Lost Cause mentality that placed white women—and southern domestic life—at the center of their thinking. Lost Cause speakers paid tribute to southern wives and mothers who "waged a battle greater than any fought on land or sea" and who displayed a heroism "even greater and grander than that of the soldiers who fell in the excitement of battle." How much ex-Confederates really believed that southern white women displayed a "greater and grander" heroism than soldiers is, I think, debatable. But the impulse to place women so prominently in postwar memorialization stemmed, I would argue, from a desire to portray the southern cause as moral, virtuous, and righteous, to signal that the Confederate commitment had always placed time-honored concerns for women and families central. Moreover, if—as Lost Causers emphasized—the war was not about slavery and slavery was, in fact, a kind and benevolent institution, white women also had critical roles to play in the re-imagining of antebellum plantation society. Slavery, after all, was not about a grueling work regimen in which profits were built on the backs of black laborers. It was, instead, a domestic arrangement in which slaves contributed to the charming home and family life of the South, and formed special attachments to white women. As the Lost Cause literature suggested, so deep was the loyalty and affection that slaves felt for white women, they could repeatedly be found as their protectors and defenders against Yankee invaders. Perhaps, too, it was this supposedly unique domestic bond formed between slaves and white women that enabled white women to become some of the supreme interpreters of this imaginary slave experience in the late-nineteenth-century South. UDC women performed "old darkey hymns," recited "Old Mammy" monologues, and spoke in the language of "black dialect" in recounting their stories of the past.[8]

But if the Lost Cause rested implicitly and sometimes explicitly on the subtext of benign slavery, in its most essential form it emphasized the Confederacy as a home-oriented movement, an enterprise clearly devoid of politics because it rested so deeply on domestic life. Nothing better captured this than an article that appeared in an 1894 issue of the *Confederate Veteran* magazine. As the story went, a southern boy and his mother attended a New York theater production of a Civil War play. When the son asks his mother why the Yankees fought, the mother replies, "For the Union, darling." The orchestra plays martial music associated with the Union cause, bringing pain to the mother's face. "What did the Confederates fight for?" the boy now asks. Taking her cue from the orchestral rendition of "Home Sweet Home," the mother answers, "Do you hear what they are playing? That is what the Confederates fought for, darling." Faced with such an obvious choice, the boy makes his own sympathies clear. "Oh mother," he declares, "I will be a Confederate." Indeed, we might ask, who wouldn't be a Confederate when being a Confederate meant holding dear those things—home, mother—that any boy might cherish?[9]

This was a mentality that doubly enshrined the icon of Confederate womanhood. In her responses, the mother of this story echoed the language of the 1860s: the Confederacy, as originally conceived, placed home and, by extension, women, central to its mission. Of course, even in the 1860s, that language obscured the South's political objectives regarding the preservation and expansion of slavery. But it was a language that proved to have an enduring popularity, resurrected as it was in the Lost Cause ideal that insisted that the Confederate objective was, once again, not about politics, or slavery, or even constitutional principles, but about women and the home. As such, it became possible to remember the South's struggle in a highly romantic light, and as a cause with which even northerners could sympathize. This kind of Lost Cause literature, with white women placed prominently as the upholders of the Confederate cause, became a staple of both northern and southern postwar writing, from the late-nineteenth-century Civil War novels of northern author John DeForest to the epic renderings, in the 1930s, of Atlanta-born Margaret Mitchell.

Yet understanding the power of this home-oriented ideology also requires some consideration of how the very meaning and symbolism associated with "home" had shifted from the wartime to the postwar years. As the scholar Grace Hale has observed, Lost Cause promoters, especially women, consistently "participated in the conflation of new middle-class home and old plantation household." To put this another way, Confederate memorializers enshrined the white South's commitment to the values of "home," but the "home" that Confederate soldiers pledged themselves to protect in the 1860s was a far cry from the "home" that was sentimentalized in the "Home Sweet Home" story of the 1890s. By the late nineteenth century, the southern economy was no longer organized around plantation households—those broadly conceived economic units that brought together the work, done by both white and black dependents, in the home and in the fields—but instead by the increasing separation, physically and ideologically, between home and work that had long been characteristic of the North. Even more, the "home" of the late-nineteenth-century South no longer entailed the ownership of human property, as it did in the antebellum era. Thus when Lost Causers celebrated the Confederate commitment to "home," they may have echoed the language used by a previous generation of southerners, but they spoke a word that was thoroughly steeped in the idealized sentimentality that Americans, especially northerners, had been using to describe the domestic sphere since the 1830s. It was a sentimentality, we might add, that had rarely embraced, and in fact was sometimes hostile to, southern slavery. As a result, when white southerners in the late nineteenth century fondly recalled the struggle for "home," they allowed all who endorsed that cause, northern and southern alike, to further obscure the central place of slavery in the Confederate cause.[10]

It should hardly be surprising, then, that when ex-Confederates spoke tearfully of their fight for "home sweet home," they spoke in a language that captured the sentiments, and the politics, of many white southerners. The historian general of the United Daughters of the Confederacy ably captured the conservative political impulse and romantic idealism of that sentiment when she spoke before a Washington, DC, audience in 1912. Mildred Rutherford insisted that there was no rupture from the antebellum South to the South of today and that just as the southern women of the past influenced their surroundings from the vantage point of their homes, so they would continue to do so. "If there is a power that is placed in any hands," she intoned, "it is the power that is placed in the Southern woman in her home." No matter that the woman of the antebellum South exercised far less power, even over the home, than her postbellum descendants: Rutherford's remarks spoke to the sustaining and continuing power of the South's domestic ideal, apparently unchanged in the revolutionary transformation from the slavery to the postslavery era.[11]

White northerners, too, felt the pull of this sentiment almost as much as southerners. Immersed in their own culture that romanticized the domestic sphere, northerners found the story of Confederates fighting, above all else, for homes and families, a moving and inspiring one and eventually adopted it as their version of Civil War history. In hundreds of ways, northerners helped give that story the stamp of legitimacy. For example, curators at the newly established United States National Museum (later part of the Smithsonian Institution) hoped, in the 1880s, to acquire "home made shoes and homespun cloth" from the late Confederacy, items that could "illustrate the privations and poverty endured throughout the South during the war" and thereby emblematize the domestic component of the southern war effort. Sympathy for the Confederacy's domestic plight also encouraged northerners to collaborate with their southern colleagues in placing southern white women central to their Civil War memories, whether in fiction, drama, or historical accounts. In part, the notion of the feminized South, as I have argued elsewhere, offered white northerners a safer and more acceptable path to postwar reconciliation than a reunion that demanded an alliance with southern men. Thus the widely rehearsed formula, prevalent in so much postwar fiction, imagined the reunification of the nation from the perspective of a domestic union between a northern man and a southern woman. As such, it was a formula that clearly acknowledged northern political and economic dominance. But it nonetheless conceded sentiment and feminine virtues to the South. Certainly the conciliatory impulse motivated federal politicians to make a Washington, DC, monument, initially proposed as a tribute to Union women, a site that would honor women of the North and South. By 1917, the year of the memorial's dedication, southern sensibilities had, in effect, hijacked the project: Senator John Williams of Mississippi, the principal orator at the dedication, delivered a tribute that focused almost exclusively on the women of Dixie.[12]

Yet if Williams's words set the tone for what had initially been imagined as a cross-sectional tribute, he could take comfort in the fact that few northerners would have objected to his southern bias. So strong was northern devotion to southern womanhood that northern observers, on their own, frequently identified southern women as the feminine superiors of their Yankee counterparts. This, in effect, represented another version of the Lost Cause conflation of "home" and plantation household, only now Yankees, in their haste to hold up the South as a domestic model for all Americans, essentially imprinted an idealized image of the antebellum plantation mistress upon the countenance of late-nineteenth-century southern women. As a character in one northern magazine story explained, "Our Southern ladies . . . thoroughly understand the art of housekeeping" and "never dreamed of anything but politeness or consideration." Given the old South's tradition of elevating its "ladies," as much as possible, from the day-to-day obligations of "housekeeping," it seems remarkable that southern women would rank so highly in this regard. Indeed, this image of southern womanhood probably spoke more to the idealized representations of the antebellum North's domestic sphere than to anything that ever existed in the antebellum South. Nonetheless, it was a representation that seemed—sadly to many in the North—no longer applicable to the striving, aggressive, and independent women of Yankeedom.[13]

Finally, the numerical presence of southern white women *in* Confederate commemoration can offer, in itself, an explanation for the far more extensive memorialization *of* Confederate women on the southern landscape. Put simply, southern white women were in a better position than northern women to make themselves the objects of remembrance. The orator, for example, who extolled southern women for displaying a "greater and grander" heroism than Confederate soldiers presided over the Mississippi chapter of the United Daughters of the Confederacy and delivered her remarks at the dedication of a monument to Confederate women in Jackson, Mississippi. In South Carolina, the women who belonged to the Wade Hampton chapter of the UDC made it a priority to compile a historical volume that would call attention to the active and productive contributions South Carolina women made during the Civil War. Impressed by women's efforts in memorial work, southern white men also constructed monuments to Confederate women that partly commemorated wartime labors but also paid tribute to women's postwar contributions as well, something that may have been uppermost in their minds in the 1890s and early 1900s when these monuments were being built. Along these lines, the statue that Confederate veterans constructed to honor the Confederate women of South Carolina called greater attention to the postwar than to the

J. K. Tillotson, a playwright of the late nineteenth century, drew on the popular formula of intersectional romance for his 1883 play, "The Planter's Wife." Although dramatists usually paired a southern woman with a northern man, Tillotson varied the formula slightly by making the plantation mistress a woman born in the North but now inhabiting the apparently traditional role of the southern lady. (Billy Rose Theatre Division, The New York Public Library for the Performing Arts, Astor, Lenox, and Tilden Foundations)

wartime period, observing that women's "virtues stood as the supreme citadel" in "the rebuilding after the desolation."[14]

Yet, despite the persistent celebration of traditional feminine virtues, southern white women did not remain wedded to the same traditional gender roles of the Civil War era. Situated as they were at the helm of this hugely significant movement of remembering, southern women gained attention and influence, and cultivated connections, that they could use to promote themselves in other ways. To some extent, their participation in this southernwide movement, and their work in presenting a Confederate-wide identity, elevated southern white women from the highly localized sphere of thinking and acting that dominated the wartime period. If, to paraphrase

*In 1912 white men and women in Columbia, South Carolina, attended a
dedication ceremony for a monument, commissioned by Confederate veterans, that
paid homage to the women of South Carolina for their support of their men during
the Civil War and for their work in the postwar era. (Courtesy of the South
Caroliniana Library, University of South Carolina, Columbia)*

Robert Penn Warren, the Confederacy gained a life in the postwar
period that it had never had while it existed, then southern white
women, too, found a way to attach themselves to this legacy in a
way that allowed them to greatly expand their own sphere of influence. Just by moving from local memorial societies into the United
Daughters of the Confederacy, southern women found themselves
on a stage that had considerably greater visibility than anything they
had previously known. Moreover, as historian Fitzhugh Brundage
has argued, southern white women frequently used their positions as
memorializers and commemorators as a springboard to other social
causes. They drew on a constructed memory of the Confederacy in
campaigning for a diverse range of issues such as prohibition, public
assistance for impoverished Confederate widows and children, edu-
cational reform, and even suffrage. Not surprisingly, Confederate
memorial work also laid the groundwork that allowed southern
white women to actively advocate racial segregation and black politi-

cal disenfranchisement, although some registered opposition to the more radical expressions of southern Jim Crow. Indeed, in trying to recall Confederate women's work as active and public and vital—as opposed to the passive and prayerful images that men preferred— southern white women used Confederate commemorative work as a subtle challenge to some of the most entrenched patriarchal practices of southern society. By the early twentieth century, when Confederate veterans tried to launch a campaign to erect monuments to Confederate women throughout the South, some of the fiercest objections came from the United Daughters of the Confederacy, who believed women would now be better served by tributes—like college scholarships—that recognized their potential for present-day achievements.[15]

IN STARK CONTRAST TO THEIR Confederate counterparts, Unionist women were strikingly silent and unseen in postwar commemoration. Scant literature documented their trials and travails, and few monuments and memorials paid them tribute. Certainly their relative distance (at least for women living in the North) from the war itself partly explains the void. Because northern women were seldom caught in the crossfire and rarely subjected to wartime invasion, their story lacked much of the drama that swirled around their Confederate sisters. But if this helps explain the absence of northern women from postwar cultural offerings, it does not really explain the relatively poor visibility of Union women in northerners' postwar commemorations, either as actors or as objects of remembrance.

As was true for so many southern women, the immediate postwar period saw many northern women, as well as men, consumed by grief and suffering. Although northern society was not as devastated as the South, and did not endure nearly the same percentage of fatalities, women here nonetheless confronted loss on a scale not previously experienced. An overwhelming sense of women's grief thus pervades one of the most popular novels to emerge at the end of the Civil War, Elizabeth Stuart Phelps's *The Gates Ajar*, published in 1868. In a story that apparently paralleled some of Phelps's own wartime experiences, the young heroine of the book—Mary Cabot—confronts the death of a loved one during the war and then searches for some type of spiritual solace for her anguish. Finding the words of the official church leaders inadequate, Mary ultimately finds comfort from the more emotionally responsive religion of other women. *The Gates Ajar* says little about the war itself or about women's contributions, but it does acknowledge the unique burden borne by women in enduring the war's destruction, a theme Phelps returned to in subsequent fiction. Phelps later explained how she wrote *The Gates Ajar* with this in mind—to speak to "the helpless, outnumbering, unconsulted women" of the 1860s. Her work thus captured the emotional turmoil experienced by many women—North and South—at the war's conclusion, but it also made women's wartime, and postwar, story a very private one. Moreover, Phelps's reference to "unconsulted" women carried the suggestion that the war, aside from the suffering it brought, had little meaning or significance for women. Hence the book would have hardly directed attention toward remembering and celebrating northern women's wartime accomplishments, nor motivating northern women themselves into taking up commemorative public work.[16]

Not that Union women's commemorative efforts were completely negligible. Unionist women did organize and they did commemorate. Sometimes, even, they were commemorated. A few celebratory volumes—hailing women's contributions as nurses and aid workers—appeared right after the war's conclusion. A few women who became active in late-nineteenth-century social movements—suffrage, temperance, social welfare—also looked back to their own, and other northern women's, Civil War experiences in order to make a case for women's emerging patriotism and activism. Women, they argued, had answered the nation's call in shouldering the economic demands of the home front and the relief efforts for the military, but the nation had failed to fully acknowledge women for the contributions they made. Former Sanitary Commission leader Mary Livermore published her wartime reminiscences in 1887 because she believed that the story of "the consecrated and organized work of women, who strengthened the sinews of the nation with their unflagging enthusiasm" had yet to be "fully narrated." Even more, as an active lecturer for women's suffrage in the late nineteenth century, Livermore would have been keenly aware of the nation's continuing neglect and disregard of women's civic contributions, present as well as past. Directing their Civil War remembrances toward an argument on behalf of late-nineteenth-century women's rights, female memoirists like Livermore maintained that despite heroic, wartime sacrifices, women wrongly continued to receive second-class treatment.[17]

But perhaps the most sustained work undertaken by northern women for the purpose of memorializing the Union war effort was done through the female auxiliary groups attached to Union veterans' organizations. Soon after the war, women began participating in these societies, merging them together in 1883 to form the Woman's Relief Corps (WRC), the principal female auxiliary to the nation's largest veterans' group, the Grand Army of the Republic (GAR). By 1894, the WRC counted 118,000 members, making it the second-largest distinct women's organization (the Woman's Christian Temperance Union was first) in the late nineteenth century. WRC work, at least in some respects, resembled the efforts of the ladies memorial associations in the South, and later the UDC. They decorated the graves of Civil War soldiers and helped to organize the annual Memorial Day commemorations when veterans and their supporters would walk to local cemeteries, place flowers on graves, and listen to speakers who recalled the heroic work accomplished by the Union soldier.[18]

Yet, in a number of ways, WRC and GAR efforts conspired to make Union women far less noticeable in the northern memory of the Civil War than southern women were in Confederate memories. Although women who joined the Woman's Relief Corps did not ignore commemorative activities, they also did not prioritize that work like their pro-Confederate sisters. Local chapters of the WRC typically devoted most of their efforts, and budgets, to identifying veterans and veterans' widows and children in economic need. The Lincoln, Illinois, chapter of the WRC spent considerable time in

Apparently wearing the insignia of their organization, these members of the Gunnison, Colorado, Woman's Relief Corps, the main women's auxiliary to the Grand Army of the Republic, posed for this group portrait sometime in the 1890s. (Denver Public Library, Western History Collection, x-9284)

distributing relief to needy families, raising contributions for a local soldiers' hospital, and arranging to place children from an indigent veteran's family in a nearby Soldiers' Children's Home. They devoted, in contrast, surprisingly little emphasis to memorial work and did little, if anything, to promote the construction of commemorative monuments. In reporting on local activities to the national convention, the members of a Tennessee chapter of the WRC explained that there had been some interest there in building a monument to Union women but they had decided against this because they believed their primary obligation was to care for "the needy veteran and his family."[19]

What might account for these different points of emphasis in how Union and pro-Confederate women chose to spend their time and their money? Certainly Confederate veterans and their families could have used some economic relief, probably even more so than Union ones who, depending on their circumstances, might at least turn to the federal pension system for some measure of support. But perhaps because northern veterans had learned to train their sights on pensions, northern women may have also had a heightened awareness of suffering among those who either did not receive adequate pensions or did not qualify to receive them. (In fact, before 1890, only widows of soldiers who had died from service-related wounds or diseases were eligible for pensions.) Thus, the WRC, no doubt encouraged by the GAR, may have identified one of their primary responsibilities as filling in the gaps where the pension system did not go. Along these lines, it is noteworthy that the WRC vigorously campaigned, ultimately with some limited success, for federal pensions for U.S. Army nurses. The campaign did, in fact, require WRC women to recall and highlight female nurses' wartime contributions, but ultimately they aimed not so much at memorializing Union nurses—in the form of tributes or monuments—but at winning them monetary compensation. Confederate women, unable to make claims for money, instead focused their efforts on memory.[20]

The class composition of the northern and southern groups might also explain the reasons why the two spent their money so differently. Southern groups tended to draw predominantly from the social elite, from women married to some of the wealthiest businessmen and most prominent Confederate officers of their communities. As such, they may have been relatively unaware of the needs of those less economically privileged, or had suspicions about how pressing their needs really were. The WRC had, in contrast, a more economically diverse membership and, no doubt, came in closer contact with less privileged members of their communities. Finally, Union women may have felt that monument-building was less pressing than other tasks precisely because they lived in a culture and a society that did not challenge the cause for which they and their men had fought or inflict restrictions on their celebratory rituals. Southern white women, on the other hand, felt the need to challenge not only Reconstruction officials' perception of who did, and did not, deserve to be honored among the wartime dead, but also black southerners' attempts to hold their own public, commemorative displays in support of the Union and emancipation. In the North, however, Union women chose to remember the Union legacy not with signs and symbols that would stand out to contemporary observers but with smaller monetary disbursements to those deemed deserving of their support.[21]

On a broader, ideological level, the cause that Unionists remembered and celebrated also served to push northern women into the background of Civil War memory while it simultaneously encouraged women, and men, to glorify the work of the needy, and the not so needy, veteran. Union commemoration, to put it simply, privileged the saving of the Union and the men who had accomplished that task. Whereas Confederate memorialization demanded a recognition of women and the home as the apparently neutral embodiments of the Lost Cause, Union commemoration—not unlike Union men's wartime ideology—placed foremost attention on the nation, as an objective distinct from homes and families. The story of the southern boy and his mother at the theater captured the essential difference between the two memorial traditions and the central problem Union women faced in postwar remembrances: if, as the southern mother tells her son, the Yankees fought to save the Union, there was not really a place—or at least not a very visible one—for northern women in the postwar Union imagination. Surely, as many Memorial Day speakers acknowledged, northern women had assisted the men in their work. But saving the Union, at least as it was frequently remembered, was ultimately men's business, not women's, and it was a business that lacked the sentimental and feminine influences that surrounded the Lost Cause. Thus in commemorative speeches and activities, women were, often quite literally, shoved to the sidelines. Recognizing the Union widows and children in attendance at an 1889 Memorial Day event, a Michigan speaker described their subordinate status, much as Union soldiers in the 1860s had emphasized the subordination of home and family to the demands of the nation. "They came here," he explained, "not to mourn, but to bow down and worship before the shrine of liberty, and acknowledge the sacrifice which was made for them and future generations." The members of a California WRC chapter declined a GAR invitation to march in their parade, preferring to stay "on the sidewalks" and cheer for "their fathers, brothers, sons and lovers."[22]

The marginalizing of Union veterans' wives drew the attention, in the early twentieth century, of Elizabeth Stuart Phelps, now at the end of a long career of authorship. In her 1911 short story, "Comrades," the author of *The Gates Ajar* described the efforts of an aged Union veteran, and his wife, as he struggles to attend what may be his last Memorial Day event. Weak and infirm, the veteran wishes his wife could march beside him. "But you ain't a veteran," he tells her. Reflecting on her own struggles to support him and their family, during and after the war, she replies, "I don't know about that." Ultimately, the soldier, the only surviving veteran in his community, begins the procession on his own while his wife—following the tradition of other veterans' female relatives—chooses to walk to the side, "without offense to the ceremonies." But when he almost stumbles, she joins him in the final march, and they officially become the "comrades" in the story's title. "What'll folks say?" the aged soldier cries. "They'll say I'm where I belong," she replies. "I've earned the right to." Hoping to give notice to the trials and endurance of the old soldier's spouse, Phelps captured the degree to which Union veterans' wives had long been the unseen and unacknowledged partners in the Union struggle, and in the effort to honor its legacy.[23]

Phelps reflected critically on Union women's marginalized status, but the Woman's Relief Corps seemed to accept the tradition that kept women to the side. Yet, in other ways, the WRC embraced a more robust notion of women's political expressiveness, specifically in claiming the Unionist legacy of female patriotism and the notion that all individuals, women as well as men, must take responsibility for their own political positions. During wartime, this had translated into an insistence, on women's part, to ground their patriotism in a political and ideological defense of the Union, not simply on unswerving support for male kin. It had also translated into an insistence that Confederate women pay the price for their own treason and take responsibility for their own declarations of loyalty, or really disloyalty. In the postwar era, the Woman's Relief Corps drew on this legacy of female patriotism in defining its membership criteria. Unlike its smaller rival organization—the Ladies of the Grand Army of the Republic—the WRC insisted that any "loyal woman" could join their society, not just those who were related to Union soldiers or GAR veterans. In this way, the WRC broke with an older conception of female patriotism and instead judged women as loyal, or not, on the basis of their own actions and viewpoints. "The relatives of the Union veteran," argued the WRC's president in 1887, "have no right to trade on an excess of loyalty and to arrogate to themselves all the patriotism of the women of our land." Women, they argued, demonstrated their loyalty not by marriage but by individual allegiance. This included army nurses, most of whom "had no tie of blood in husband, son, father or brother" and acted only out of "the divine instinct of humanity and their undying loyalty to principle and country." This even included women married to, or related to, Confederates. "Each applicant," the organization's leaders insisted, "stands on her own record in regard to loyalty."[24]

The emphasis on personal loyalty had significant consequences for WRC work and for the WRC membership. For one, it opened the doors of the organization, in not insignificant ways, to African American women. With loyalty, and not race, as the principal criteria, both white and black women in the WRC insisted on bringing black women into their ranks, sometimes over the objections of southern white members of the organization, and thereby honoring the patriotic legacy of African Americans in the Civil War. "The negroes over the country," explained a black member of a Washington, DC, chapter, "are as loyal now as they were in '61 and '65." In a number of southern states, black women played prominent roles in the organization, although they generally did so through segregated local chapters. In Kentucky, for example, thirty-two local chapters were African American, compared to ten that were white. The numerical discrepancy prompted outcries from southern white women who insisted that other white women would not join a black-dominated group. While the WRC leadership sometimes bowed to white pressure to remove the black chapters from the jurisdiction of white-dominated state organizations, they generally held firm to the principle of black membership. Indeed, in chapters in Wisconsin, black and white women joined integrated locals and worked together on various WRC initiatives, including, in at least one instance, extending aid to "a colored family in need."[25]

No doubt WRC members would have found numerous African American families, even veterans' families, "in need." Although, in theory, black Union soldiers and their families were entitled to federal pensions, many African Americans found it difficult to surmount the numerous bureaucratic and sometimes explicitly racist obstacles that stood between them and their pension allotments. Indeed, some black women may have turned to the Woman's Relief Corps because it offered some measure of financial assistance for funerals and might give aid to African American families who suffered financial hardship. Some women, too, may have hoped that in joining the WRC they could avail themselves of a network of women who had experience in securing pensions for veterans and their kin.

But in the South, black women were no doubt motivated by more than economic imperatives when they participated in Civil War commemorative organizations and activities. The power of the Confederate tradition certainly inspired some black women to find ways to honor the black Civil War legacy with more visible signs and symbols. A Virginia chapter of the WRC, for example, planned to raise money for a monument to black soldiers buried in the "colored" section of a Norfolk cemetery. More often, black southerners found it difficult to secure adequate funding and space for monuments and so preferred to hold public ceremonies and parades on days set aside for celebrating the end of slavery. Sometimes these events drew on Woman's Relief Corps members, but the principal organizers were more likely to come from other civic, religious, and commercial groups in the black community. Choosing to highlight the black Civil War experience in such public venues, and seeking to counter potential white hostility, black southerners placed a premium on proving themselves as respectable and upstanding members of their towns and cities. As such, black women played a critical part in being highly visible on these occasions, their very presence a testament to the manners and decorum of the black community. But without the resources that would allow them to create permanent tributes, black women's visibility in Civil War commemoration would, of necessity, be momentary and temporary.[26]

There were other ways, besides monuments, that black women might call attention to African Americans' central place in the Civil War, and to the unique contributions of black women themselves. Susie King Taylor, ex-slave, former wartime nurse, and active member of the Massachusetts Woman's Relief Corps, spotlighted her own wartime contributions, especially in teaching and caring for black Union regiments in the South Carolina Sea Islands, when she compiled and published her reminiscences in 1902. Onetime abolitionist Frances Ellen Harper likewise called attention to black women's work as nurses, teachers, and unofficial spies for the Union army when she wrote her 1892 novel, *Iola Leroy*. Harper's widely read story covered the years before, during, and after the war and was told from the point of view of a light-skinned African American woman who gradually learns of her racial heritage. The book represented Harper's attempt to refute the more general erasure of black women from wartime remembrances and the Lost Cause distortion of the African American experience. Taking a pointed jab at the scant attention paid to the slaves and their descendants in the historical record, Harper has one character in *Iola Leroy* even make a plea that some future and "faithful historian will chronicle all the deeds of daring and service" rendered by ordinary black women and men for the Union army.[27]

The writings of Susie King Taylor, as well as Frances Harper, remained true to the spirit of the Woman's Relief Corps with its emphasis on paying tribute to all who were, and remained, loyal to the Union war effort, whether they were white or black, male or female. Yet, increasingly, the focus on loyalty pushed the WRC away from the sphere of Civil War remembrance altogether. Perhaps because they had not limited their membership solely to the relatives of

Although some black women joined the Woman's Relief Corps, more would have commemorated the Civil War through activities like the one pictured here, a 1905 Emancipation Day celebration in Richmond, Virginia. (Library of Congress, Prints and Photographs Division, Detroit Publishing Company Collection)

Union veterans, the WRC had opened its ranks to a wider group of women who, while they might define themselves as "loyal," did not feel the need to ground that loyalty solely in the Civil War past. In any event, the organization over time showed less interest in affirming the Unionist position and more with disseminating a patriotic commitment to the United States among a growing population—in the northern states especially—of foreigners and immigrants. "Loyalty," proclaimed the WRC president in 1887, "is inherent in many, is a process of growth in others, and 'to inculcate its teaching in the communities in which we live' should be the aim of every patriotic woman." In this way, the WRC carved itself a new niche in Gilded Age America: to teach and inculcate "patriotic" values among children and immigrants by distributing flags, sponsoring essay contests, and promoting a recently composed "pledge of allegiance" to the

U.S. flag. By the 1890s, many in the WRC would have concluded that the more pressing danger that lay ahead in the fight for patriotism came not from Lost Causers but from immigrants who knew little about American history and American traditions. In the early twentieth century, the Woman's Relief Corps would join forces with other patriotic women—in groups like the Daughters of the American Revolution—sounding the alarm against anarchism, bolshevism, and trade unionism.[28]

And so, the choices made by Unionist and pro-Confederate women in the 1870s, 1880s, and 1890s have bequeathed to us a legacy that has given southern white women an exaggerated presence in our memory of the Civil War and left Union women with barely a memorial or tribute worth noticing. In this regard, the real and significant strides taken by Union women during the war have, by and large, gone unacknowledged. As I have tried to suggest, Union women, more so than their Confederate counterparts, laid claim to new civic and political identities in the course of the war, forced as they were to grapple with a set of objectives that extended far beyond their immediate hearths and homes. Northern women's wartime work helped ignite a heightened sense of civic obligation and political participation, and even encouraged, at times, a willingness to break with traditional gender practices if that was the price to be paid in sacrificing for the Union. That legacy of expanding civic and political work endured long after the Civil War had ended, despite the fading memories that many had regarding Union women's actual Civil War experiences.

Indeed, well into the postwar era, northern women continued to shape an even keener sense of civic engagement and fashion an even sharper political identity, ultimately forging a critical collaboration with the federal government as they championed Progressive Era demands for suffrage and social welfare. Yet they did so largely through venues outside the realm of Civil War commemoration—in organizations focused on temperance, on urban reform, and on gaining the right to vote. In some respects, in fact, close affiliation with veterans' societies may have been a political liability for both the men and the women engaged in that work. As the scholar Theda Skocpol has suggested, those who were in any way associated with the campaign to secure Civil War pensions, whether male or female, found their political status—by the end of the nineteenth century—more and more compromised by the taint of patronage and corruption that swarmed around the pension movement. Hence women in groups like the Woman's Relief Corps, who focused their energies on Union soldiers' pensions, may have had less political clout than northern women in groups that had no relationship to Civil War commemoration.[29]

In contrast, southern white women may have found in Confederate remembrance work the single most important springboard into the public arena. Because this work provided a socially acceptable venue for assuming public authority, and because it so often championed women's vital contributions to civic enterprises, Confederate commemoration opened doors for southern white women into a vast array of Progressive Era reforms. Significantly, too, it also oriented southern white women—more often than not—to promote the coming tide of segregation and racial oppression, hailed by many in the New South as yet another forward-looking innovation of the modern era. Perhaps many of the Civil War generation, on the Confederate side (and perhaps even on the Union side), would have applauded the new racial order. Still, one final conclusion, I think, suggests itself from all of this: by promoting the memory of the Confederacy in the post-Confederate era, and by doing so in such a public and visible way, southern white women took steps toward political activism that signaled a dramatic rupture with the old South's patriarchal tradition and that, most likely, would have shocked and appalled the very Confederate leaders who were the objects of their commemoration.

Epilogue

Well into the twentieth century, southern white women continued to capture the imagination of American readers, moviegoers, and even scholars. Yet, by the early part of the twentieth century, the charming and domestic belle of nineteenth-century popular culture had undergone some noteworthy transformations. Much of the change could be attributed to the work of Margaret Mitchell, who, in her portrait of Scarlett O'Hara, may have done more than any other individual to secure the iconic place of the southern white woman. Mitchell's success had everything to do with her ability to complicate the picture of the generally one-dimensional nineteenth century belle and to create something new, even "modern," in her portrait of the scheming and determined Scarlett. Mitchell's protagonist, after all, wins our attention not because she is innocent and morally upright but because she is sexual, ambitious, and decidedly ambivalent about Victorian morality. Scarlett adopts some of the pretenses of southern ladyhood, but they are clearly, for her, only pretenses. She loudly proclaims her romantic objectives, not to mention her financial ones, throughout the period of the war and its aftermath. By recreating the southern belle in a twentieth-century context, Mitchell managed to give the southern woman of the Civil War era a new lease on life and created a female character whose presence would reverberate for decades to come. Thousands of American women, also negotiating the boundaries between ladylike decorum and modern-day selfhood, found much that was relevant in Scarlett's own dilemmas. Even Japanese tourists in late-twentieth-century Atlanta have gone in search of Scarlett; and they have found her, as the journalist Tony Horwitz has told us, in modern, kitschy, yet somehow resonant, recreations.[1]

While Scarlett occupies ground zero in Civil War–oriented popular culture, battles and soldiers and generals continue to occupy the dominant space on Civil War bookshelves. The Civil War, after all, *was* a war and so, understandably, the military components of that war continue to draw the attention of popular and academic historians. Civil War buffs don't generally become buffs because of their interest in female arsenal workers or even seamstresses who labored long and hard to sew a regimental flag. They want to know how battles were fought, why so many men enlisted, why so many men died, why some battles were Union victories and why others were won by the outnumbered and undersupplied Confederates.

But as numerous scholars have begun to suggest, it has become increasingly difficult to ignore questions related to female arsenal workers or seamstresses, even for those who seek a greater understanding of the military conflict. This present volume has aimed to draw upon and build upon this scholarship, to explain how and why gender matters to our view of the Civil War, how it matters for understanding why men enlisted, how it even makes a difference—even if it is not decisive—in understanding the variety of factors that led to victories and defeats. Even more, I have called extra attention to northern women and to understandings of gender as it affected both the men and women who supported the Union cause, especially because this has been such a sorely overlooked aspect of Civil War history. Gender gave a particular cast to men's and women's understanding of the Union cause, an understanding that not only shaped the reasons men enlisted but may have even affected the ideological climate that ultimately made Union success possible. Likewise, understandings of gender and female autonomy also created a different kind of political climate for women in the North, one that helped advance modern political notions of individualism and political accountability. And yet, perhaps ironically, some of these same notions of gender conspired in the postwar period to erase the memories of northern women's wartime contributions and to focus exaggerated attention on the experiences of southern white women. Like other scholars who have turned their attention to northern women, I hope this work manages, to some extent, to put northern women back into a story that has focused largely on battlefield maneuvers and Scarlett O'Hara's troubled and tortuous love life.

Notes

Preface

1. Recent works examining gender and the Civil War include Drew Faust, *Mothers of Invention: Women of the Slaveholding South in the American Civil War* (Chapel Hill: University of North Carolina Press, 1996); Elizabeth Leonard, *All the Daring of the Soldier: Women of the Civil War Armies* (New York: W. W. Norton, 1999); Catherine Clinton, *Tara Revisited: Women, War, and the Plantation Legend* (New York: Abbeville Press, 1995); Laura Edwards, *Scarlett Doesn't Live Here Anymore: Southern Women in the Civil War Era* (Urbana: University of Illinois Press, 2000); J. Matthew Gallman, *America's Joan of Arc: The Life of Anna Elizabeth Dickinson* (New York: Oxford University Press, 2006); Jeanie Attie, *Patriotic Toil: Northern Women and the American Civil War* (Ithaca, NY: Cornell University Press, 1998); Leslie Schwalm, *A Hard Fight for We: Women's Transition from Slavery to Freedom in South Carolina* (Urbana: University of Illinois Press, 1997); Tera Hunter, *To 'Joy My Freedom: Southern Black Women's Lives and Labors After the Civil War* (Cambridge, MA: Harvard University Press, 1997); Elizabeth Varon, *Southern Lady, Yankee Spy: The True Story of Elizabeth Van Lew, A Union Agent in the Heart of the Confederacy* (New York: Oxford University Press, 2003); Carol Bleser and Lesley Gordon, *Intimate Strategies of the Civil War: Military Commanders and Their Wives* (New York: Oxford University Press, 2001); and Nina Silber, *Daughters of the Union: Northern Women Fight the Civil War* (Cambridge, MA: Harvard University Press, 2005). I refer here to the argument advanced by Drew Faust in "Altars of Sacrifice: Confederate Women and the Narratives of War," in *Divided Houses: Gender and the Civil War*, ed. Catherine Clinton and Nina Silber (New York: Oxford University Press, 1992), in which she argues that because of the way in which the Civil War failed to address the interests and concerns of southern white women that "[i]t may well have been because of its women that the South lost the Civil War" (199).

2. Numerous arguments—aside from Faust's—have been advanced to ex-

plain why the Confederacy lost the Civil War. Among those arguments are Gary Gallagher, *The Confederate War: How Popular Will, Nationalism, and Military Strategy Could Not Stave Off Defeat* (Cambridge, MA: Harvard University Press, 1997); William Frehling, *The South vs. the South: How Anti-Confederate Southerners Shaped the Course of the Civil War* (New York: Oxford University Press, 2001); Herman Hattaway and Archer Jones, *How the North Won: A Military History of the Civil War* (Urbana: University of Illinois Press, 1983); and Kenneth Stampp, "The Southern Road to Appomattox," in Kenneth Stampp, *The Imperiled Union: Essays on the Background of the Civil War* (New York: Oxford University Press, 1980). LeeAnn Whites, "The Civil War as a Crisis in Gender," in Clinton and Silber, eds., *Divided Houses*, 3–21.

3. Whites, "The Civil War as a Crisis in Gender," 3–21. The literature on war and gender dislocations includes Margaret Randolph Higonnet et al., eds., *Behind the Lines: Gender and the Two World Wars* (New Haven: Yale University Press, 1987); Jean Bethke Elshtain, *Women and War* (New York: Basic Books, 1987); Lynn Hunt, *The Family Romance of the French Revolution* (Berkeley: University of California Press, 1992).

4. Historians have addressed the centrality of slavery in the coming, and the fighting, of the Civil War in numerous studies. Among those works are Chandra Manning, *What This Cruel War Was Over: Soldiers, Slavery, and the Civil War* (New York: Knopf, 2007); Freehling, *The South vs. the South*; Leonard Richards, *The Slave Power: The Free North and Southern Domination, 1780–1860* (Baton Rouge: Louisiana State University Press, 2000); and Eric Foner, *Free Soil, Free Labor, Free Men: The Ideology of the Republican Party Before the Civil War* (New York: Oxford University Press, 1970).

5. Recent literature on the Civil War in memory includes David Blight, *Race and Reunion: The Civil War in American Memory* (Cambridge, MA: Harvard University Press, 2001); William Blair, *Cities of the Dead: Contesting the Memory of the Civil War in the South, 1865–1914* (Chapel Hill: University of North Carolina Press, 2004); John Neff, *Honoring the Civil War Dead: Commemoration and the Problem of Reconciliation* (Lawrence: University Press of Kansas, 2005); and Alice Fahs and Joan Waugh, eds., *The Memory of the Civil War in American Culture* (Chapel Hill: University of North Carolina Press, 2004).

6. Blight, *Race and Reunion*.

7. Among the works that point to complex familial and community divisions in the border region are Edward Ayers, *In the Presence of Mine Enemies: The Civil War in the Heart of America, 1859–1863* (New York: W. W. Norton,

2003), and Amy Murrell Taylor, *The Divided Family in Civil War America* (Chapel Hill: University of North Carolina Press, 2005).

Chapter One

1. *The Diary and Letters of Kathe Kollwitz*, edited by Hans Kollwitz and translated by Richard and Clara Winston (Evanston, IL: Northwestern University Press, 1988), 62.

2. James McPherson, *For Cause and Comrades: Why Men Fought in the Civil War* (New York: Oxford University Press, 1997); New York soldier quoted in James McPherson, *What They Fought For, 1861–1865* (New York: Doubleday, 1995), 34. A good general review of recent literature on Civil War soldiers can be found in Aaron Sheehan-Dean, "The Blue and the Gray in Black and White: Assessing the Scholarship on Civil War Soldiers," in *The View from the Ground: Experiences of Civil War Soldiers*, ed. Aaron Sheehan-Dean (Lexington: University Press of Kentucky, 2007). Another recent account of Civil War soldiers' ideological beliefs is Chandra Manning, *What This Cruel War Was Over: Soldiers, Slavery, and the Civil War* (New York: Knopf, 2007).

3. Robert Westbrook, "'I Want a Girl, Just like the Girl that Married Harry James': American Women and the Problem of Political Obligation in World War II," *American Quarterly* 42 (December 1990): 591.

4. Ibid., 587–614.

5. Stephanie McCurry, "Citizens, Soldiers' Wives and 'Hiley Hope Up' Slaves: The Problem of Political Obligation in the Civil War South," in *Gender and the Southern Body Politic*, ed. Nancy Bercaw (Jackson: University Press of Mississippi, 2000), 95–124; Reid Mitchell, *The Vacant Chair: The Northern Soldier Leaves Home* (New York: Oxford University Press, 1993), xi–18; soldiers quoted in McPherson, *For Cause and Comrades*, 135, and Stephanie McCurry, "'The Soldier's Wife': White Women, the State, and the Politics of Protection in the Confederacy," in *Women and the Unstable State in Nineteenth-Century America*, ed. Alison Parker and Stephanie Cole (College Station: Texas A&M University Press, 2000), 17.

6. Alice Fahs, *The Imagined Civil War: Popular Literature of the North and South, 1861–1865* (Chapel Hill: University of North Carolina Press, 2001), 120–49.

7. Samuel Osgood, "The Home and the Flag," *Harper's New Monthly Magazine*, quoted in ibid., 123.

8. New Orleans speaker quoted in George Rable, *Civil Wars: Women and the Crisis of Southern Nationalism* (Urbana: University of Illinois Press, 1989), 47; "Barbara Frietchie" quoted from and discussed in Fahs, *Imagined Civil War*, 124.

9. John and James Welsh quoted in McPherson, *For Cause and Comrades*, 14–15.

10. McPherson, *What They Fought For*, 20; McCurry, "'The Soldier's Wife'"; Elizabeth Fox-Genovese, *Within the Plantation Household: Black and White Women of the Old South* (Chapel Hill: University of North Carolina Press, 1988), 37–99.

11. Stephanie McCurry, *Masters of Small Worlds: Yeomen Households, Gender Relations, and the Political Culture of the Antebellum South Carolina Low Country* (New York: Oxford University Press, 1995), 208–38; Townsend quoted in ibid., 283. Chandra Manning agrees that Confederate soldiers made much of their obligations to women because of the way they persistently, more than Union soldiers, linked notions of manhood and slavery. See Manning, *What This Cruel War Was Over*, 11–12.

12. McCurry, "Citizens, Soldiers' Wives"; Richmond soldier quoted in ibid., 98; other Confederate soldiers quoted in McPherson, *For Cause and Comrades*, 95.

13. Stephen Berry, *All that Makes a Man* (New York: Oxford University Press, 2003), 183.

14. Drew Faust, "Altars of Sacrifice: Confederate Women and the Narratives of War," in *Divided Houses: Gender and the Civil War*, ed. Catherine Clinton and Nina Silber (New York: Oxford University Press, 1992), 175; soldier in Petersburg quoted in Lisa Laskin, "'The Army Is Not Near So Much Demoralized as the Country Is': Soldiers in the Army of Northern Virginia and the Confederate Homefront," in Sheehan-Dean, ed., *View from the Ground*, 101; *The Burial of Latané* is discussed, among other places, in Thomas J. Brown, *The Public Art of Civil War Commemoration: A Brief History with Documents* (Boston and New York: Bedford/St. Martin's, 2004), 63–65.

15. The argument regarding Confederate women's growing unwillingness to support the Confederate cause is developed in Drew Faust, *Mothers of Invention: Women of the Slaveholding South in the American Civil War* (Chapel Hill: University of North Carolina Press, 1996), 234–47; James Marten, "Fatherhood in the Confederacy: Southern Soldiers and their Children," *Journal of*

Southern History 63 (May 1997): 269–92. Virginia women's continued support for the Confederate cause is discussed in William Blair, *Virginia's Private War: Feeding Body and Soul in the Confederacy, 1861–1865* (New York: Oxford University Press, 1998), 9, 131. Lesley Gordon suggests that some couples may have managed to meld youthful idealism, personal devotion, and romantic nationalism in a way that allowed them to sustain their support for the Confederacy. See Lesley Gordon, "Courting Nationalism: The Wartime Letters of Robert G. Mitchell and Amaretto Fondren," in *Inside the Confederate Nation: Essays in Honor of Emory M. Thomas*, ed. Lesley Gordon and John Inscoe (Baton Rouge: Louisiana State University Press, 2005), 188–208. Confederate woman quoted in Faust, *Mothers of Invention*, 242.

16. McCurry, "Citizens, Soldiers' Wives," 109–10; for more on Confederate nationalism, and some of its emerging wartime contradictions, see Drew Faust, *The Creation of Confederate Nationalism: Ideology and Identity in the Civil War South* (Baton Rouge: Louisiana State University Press, 1988). More recently Anne Rubin has argued that nationalism remained a vital force among Confederates during the war and continued to hold sway with white southerners in the postwar era. For more on this see Anne Rubin, *A Shattered Nation: The Rise and Fall of the Confederacy, 1861–1868* (Chapel Hill: University of North Carolina Press, 2005).

17. McCurry, "Citizens, Soldiers' Wives," 110–18.

18. Skelton quoted in Glenn C. Altschuler and Stuart M. Blumin, *Rude Republic: Americans and their Politics in the Nineteenth Century* (Princeton, NJ: Princeton University Press, 2000), 159; all others quoted in McPherson, *For Cause and Comrades*, 23, 99.

19. Minnesota soldier quoted in McPherson, *What They Fought For*, 29–30.

20. Benedict Anderson, *Imagined Communities: Reflections on the Origin and Spread of Nationalism* (New York: Verso, 1983), 5–7; Texas soldier quoted in McPherson, *For Cause and Comrades*, 98.

21. Jeanne Boydston, *Home and Work: Housework, Wages, and the Ideology of Labor in the Early Republic* (New York: Oxford University Press, 1990).

22. Ibid., 153–59.

23. Kentucky Unionist quoted in McPherson, *For Cause and Comrades*, 23; letter of Taylor Peirce, August 20, 1862, in Richard L. Kiper, ed., *Dear Catharine, Dear Taylor: The Civil War Letters of a Union Soldier and His Wife* (Lawrence: University Press of Kansas, 2002), 24.

24. Douglass C. North, *The Economic Growth of the United States, 1790–1860* (New York: W. W. Norton, 1966), 133, 155.

25. Letter of Grace Weston, January 7, 1864, in Weston-Allen Papers, Sophia Smith Collections (SSC), Smith College, Northampton, MA; Ann Gorman Condon, ed., *Architects of Our Fortune* (San Marino, CA: Huntington Library, 2001), 118.

26. Letter of Ann Cotton, June 25, 1863, Papers of Josiah Dexter Cotton, Library of Congress, Washington, DC.

27. Letter of James Bowler, September 27, 1862, Bowler Family Papers, Minnesota Historical Society (MnHS), St. Paul, MN.

28. Ibid., September 11, 1864.

29. Letter of Elizabeth Caleff, February 9, 1862, and letter of Elizabeth (Caleff) Bowler, September 28, 1864, Bowler Family Papers, MnHS; fiancée of navy officer quoted in McPherson, *For Cause and Comrades*, 139; letter of Emeline Ritner, August 17, 1864, in Charles Larimer, ed., *Love and Valor: Intimate Civil War Letters between Captain Jacob and Emeline Ritner* (Western Springs, IL: Sigourney Press, 2000), 336.

30. Confederate journal quoted in McCurry, "Citizens, Soldiers' Wives," 121. McCurry discusses the larger question of giving slave men a domestic stake in the Confederate cause, and their freedom, in "Citizens, Soldiers' Wives," 118–24.

31. On Union efforts to convey lessons in domesticity, and patriotism, to former slaves, see Nina Silber, "'A Compound of Wonderful Potency': Women Teachers of the North in the Civil War South," in *The War Was You and Me: Civilians in the American Civil War*, ed. Joan Cashin (Princeton, NJ: Princeton University Press, 2002), 35–59.

32. Laura Edwards, *Scarlett Doesn't Live Here Anymore: Southern Women in the Civil War Era* (Urbana: University of Illinois Press, 2000), 108–10; Scott Nelson and Carol Sheriff, *A People at War: Civilians and Soldiers in America's Civil War, 1854–1877* (New York: Oxford University Press, 2007), 245.

33. Mary Ryan, *Women in Public: Between Banners and Ballots, 1825–1880* (Baltimore: Johns Hopkins University Press, 1990), 148–52; Joan Cashin, "Deserters, Civilians, and Draft Resistance in the North," in Cashin, ed., *The War Was You and Me*, 262–85.

34. A discussion of the economic troubles that beset women on the northern home front and some of the measures, including the new pension system, adopted to address this can be found in Nina Silber, *Daughters of the Union:*

Northern Women Fight the Civil War (Cambridge, MA: Harvard University Press, 2005), 41–86.

35. This is not to say that government aid to the southern poor was completely absent. William Blair argues that Virginia leaders became increasingly committed to government welfare by late 1863 when they allowed the poor to make food purchases at government-subsidized prices. Nonetheless, as Blair suggests, this policy seems to have been too little and too late. See Blair, *Virginia's Private War*, 81–107.

36. Letter of Taylor Peirce, September 21, 1862, in Kiper, ed., *Dear Catharine, Dear Taylor*, 31; Sam Evans quoted in Nelson and Sheriff, *People at War*, 247.

37. Letter of Fanny Pierce, December 15, 1861, in Thayer Family Papers, Massachusetts Historical Society, Boston, MA.

38. Ohio soldier's wife quoted in McPherson, *For Cause and Comrades*, 139; letter of Grace Weston, November 26, 1863, in Weston-Allen Papers, SSC.

Chapter Two

1. New York *Herald*, April 30, 1861; Mississippi soldier quoted in James McPherson, *For Cause and Comrades: Why Men Fought in the Civil War* (New York: Oxford University Press, 1997), 135; "Our Mothers Did So before Us," song title quoted in Drew Faust, *Mothers of Invention: Women of the Slaveholding South in the American Civil War* (Chapel Hill: University of North Carolina Press, 1996), 18.

2. Linda Kerber, *Women of the Republic: Intellect and Ideology in Revolutionary America* (New York: W. W. Norton, 1980), 15–32.

3. Ibid., 73–136.

4. "Surprised," *Harper's Weekly*, May 21, 1864, 334; Virginia woman quoted in Faust, *Mothers of Invention*, 14.

5. Edmondston quoted in George Rable, *Civil Wars: Women and the Crisis of Southern Nationalism* (Urbana: University of Illinois Press, 1989), 45; Elizabeth Varon, *Southern Lady, Yankee Spy: The True Story of Elizabeth Van Lew, A Union Agent in the Heart of the Confederacy* (New York: Oxford University Press, 2003), 60–63; *Leslie's Monthly* quoted in Kathleen Endres, "The Women's Press in the Civil War: A Portrait of Patriotism, Propaganda, and Prodding," *Civil War History* 30 (March 1984): 48–49.

6. Stone and Espy quoted in Rable, *Civil Wars*, 47, 43.

7. Drew Faust, *The Creation of Confederate Nationalism: Ideology and Identity in the Civil War South* (Baton Rouge: Louisiana State University Press, 1988). An extensive and contentious literature exists on the nature of Confederate nationalism and how much southerners sustained a nationalist ideology. In addition to Faust see Anne Rubin, *A Shattered Nation: The Rise and Fall of the Confederacy, 1861–1868* (Chapel Hill: University of North Carolina Press, 2005); John McCardell, *The Idea of a Southern Nation: Southern Nationalists and Southern Nationalism, 1830–1860* (New York: W. W. Norton, 1979); Steven Channing, "Slavery and Confederate Nationalism," in *From the Old South to the New: Essays on the Transitional South*, ed. Walter J. Fraser and Winifred B. Moore (Westport, CT: Greenwood Press, 1981); and David Potter, *The South and the Sectional Conflict* (Baton Rouge: Louisiana State University Press, 1968).

8. Northern women's relief efforts are discussed in Nina Silber, *Daughters of the Union: Northern Women Fight the Civil War* (Cambridge, MA: Harvard University Press, 2005), 162–93. Confederate women's relief efforts are discussed in Faust, *Mothers of Invention*, 23–29; New York *Herald*, April 30, 1861.

9. Letter of Elizabeth Cabot, May 5, 1861, in Box 2, Folder 19, Hugh Cabot Family Papers, Schlesinger Library, Harvard University, Cambridge, MA; Edmondston quoted in Faust, *Mothers of Invention*, 25.

10. Faust, *Mothers of Invention*, 28–29. For northern women's challenges to the United States Sanitary Commission leadership see Jeannie Attie, *Patriotic Toil: Northern Women and the American Civil War* (Ithaca, NY: Cornell University Press, 1998), 122–46.

11. Quotes from Faust, *Mothers of Invention*, 243, 244.

12. On Virginia women see William Blair, *Virginia's Private War: Feeding Body and Soul in the Confederacy, 1861–1865* (New York: Oxford University Press, 1998). On one young Confederate couple's sustained commitment to the cause see Lesley Gordon, "Courting Nationalism: The Wartime Letters of Robert G. Mitchell and Amaretto Fondren," in *Inside the Confederate Nation: Essays in Honor of Emory M. Thomas*, ed. Lesley Gordon and John Inscoe (Baton Rouge: Louisiana State University Press, 2005), 188–208; Faust, *Mothers of Invention*, 234–47.

13. New York *Herald*, January 20, 1862; New York *Herald*, September 3, 1864; Gail Hamilton, "A Call to My Countrywomen," *Atlantic Monthly* 6 (March 1863): 346; "A Few Words in Behalf of the Loyal Women of the United States

by One of Themselves" (New York, 1863), in Frank Freidel, ed., *Union Pamphlets of the Civil War*, vol. 2 (Cambridge, MA: Belknap Press of Harvard University Press, 1967), 766.

14. Hamilton, "A Call," 346.

15. On the idea that housework was "leisure" see Jeanne Boydston, *Home and Work: Housework, Wages, and the Ideology of Labor in the Early Republic* (New York: Oxford University Press, 1990), 142–63; "The Fortunes of War," *Harper's Monthly*, July 1864; and "The Russian Ball," *Harper's Weekly*, November 21, 1863.

16. Fanny Fern, "Soldiers' Wives," New York *Ledger*, November 8, 1862, 4.

17. Letter of Benjamin F. Prescott, February 12, 1863, in Papers of Anna Dickinson (microfilm), Harvard University; letter of Ann Cotton, October 2, 1864, in Papers of Josiah Dexter Cotton, Library of Congress, Washington, DC; Marjorie Ann Rogers, "An Iowa Woman in Wartime," part 2, *Annals of Iowa* 35 (Spring 1961): 605.

18. Copperhead woman quoted in Mary Ryan, *Women in Public: Between Banners and Ballots, 1825–1880* (Baltimore: Johns Hopkins University Press, 1990), 148; Jane Evans quoted in Scott Nelson and Carol Sheriff, *A People at War: Civilians and Soldiers in America's Civil War, 1854–1877* (New York: Oxford University Press, 2007), 246; New York *Herald*, July 14, 1863. Mary Ryan observes that "although women were clearly a small minority of the combatants during the July Days of 1863 (less than 10 percent of those arrested), this incident was one of the more sexually integrated political actions of the nineteenth century" (Ryan, *Women in Public*, 148).

19. Illinois sergeant quoted in McPherson, *For Cause and Comrades*, 97.

20. Documents on the Ladies' National Covenant in Frank Moore, ed., *The Rebellion Record*, vol. 2 (New York: D. Van Nostrand, 1864–68), 19–22; Mary Elizabeth Massey, *Bonnet Brigades: American Women and the Civil War* (New York: Knopf, 1966), 246.

21. Documents on the Ladies' National Covenant, 20, 23.

22. Clara Barton, Diary, in Clara Barton Papers, American Antiquarian Society, Worcester, MA.

23. Ann Gorman Condon, ed., *Architects of Our Fortune* (San Marino, CA: Huntington Library, 2001), 119–27; letter of Sophia Buchanan, January 1, 1863, in George M. Blackburn, ed., "Letters to the Front: A Distaff View of the Civil War," *Michigan History* 49 (1965): 55–56.

24. Letter of Frances Ellen Watkins Harper, 1862, American Civil War: Letters and Diaries website, <http://www.alexanderstreet2.com/cwldlive/> (accessed March 9, 2004); Truth quoted in Dorothy Sterling, *We Are Your Sisters: Black Women in the Nineteenth Century* (New York: Norton, 1984), 251–52.

25. "A Few Words in Behalf of the Loyal Women of the United States," 780, 769, 785.

26. Ibid., 780, 784.

27. Letter of Ruth A. Whittemore, June 12, 1863, in Walter Rundell Jr., ed., "'Despotism of Traitors': The Rebellious South Through New York Eyes," *New York History* 45 (October 1964): 354; Adams quoted in Evelyn Leasher, ed., *Letter from Washington, 1863–1865* (Detroit: Wayne State University Press, 1999), 262.

28. Memo of Brig. Gen. Stoughton, March 1, 1863, in *The War of the Rebellion: A Compilation of the Official Records of the Union and Confederate Armies* (CD-ROM, Carmel, IN, 1997), series 1, vol. 25, part 2, 114; for more on Rogers and his work see "Taking the Oath and Drawing Rations," at the Smithsonian American Art Museum website, <http://americanart.si.edu> (accessed on July 18, 2007).

29. Frank Klingberg, *The Southern Claims Commission* (Berkeley: University of California Press, 1955), 89–116, 147–51.

30. Remarks and proceedings from the Woman's Loyal National League appear in Elizabeth Cady Stanton, Susan B. Anthony, and Matilda Gage, eds., *History of Woman Suffrage*, vol. 2 (New York: Fowler and Wells, 1882), 51–86; Mrs. O. S. Baker, "The Ladies' Loyal League," *Continental Monthly* 4 (July 1863): 51–56.

31. Letter of Robert Hubbard, February 25, 1863, in Letters of Robert Hubbard, Civil War Manuscripts Collection, Yale University Library; letter of Taylor Peirce, May 4, 1863, in Richard L. Kiper, ed., *Dear Catharine, Dear Taylor: The Civil War Letters of a Union Soldier and His Wife* (Lawrence: University Press of Kansas, 2002), 108.

32. For more on Dickinson's wartime lecturing see J. Matthew Gallman, *America's Joan of Arc: The Life of Anna Elizabeth Dickinson* (New York: Oxford University Press, 2006), 19–43; letter of Emeline Ritner, June 26, 1864, in Charles Larimer, ed., *Love and Valor: Intimate Civil War Letters between Captain Jacob and Emeline Ritner* (Western Springs, IL: Sigourney Press, 2000); letter of Ruth Whittemore, June 19, 1863, in Rundell, ed., "'Despotism of Traitors,'" 355.

Chapter Three

1. Thomas J. Brown, *The Public Art of Civil War Commemoration: A Brief History with Documents* (New York: Bedford/St. Martin's, 2004), 58–61.

2. James McPherson has remarked on the difficulty of determining the numbers of Civil War dead, especially among southern civilians. He provides an estimated number of 50,000. See James McPherson, *Battle Cry of Freedom: The Civil War Era* (New York: Oxford University Press, 1988), 619. Among the books addressing southern white women's role in Confederate commemoration are LeeAnn Whites, *The Civil War as a Crisis in Gender: Augusta, Georgia, 1860–1890* (Athens: University of Georgia Press, 1995), 160–98; David Blight, *Race and Reunion: The Civil War in American Memory* (Cambridge, MA: Belknap Press of Harvard University Press, 2001), 272–84; William Blair, *Cities of the Dead: Contesting the Memory of the Civil War in the South, 1865–1914* (Chapel Hill: University of North Carolina Press, 2004), 77–105; and Cynthia Mills and Pamela H. Simpson, eds., *Monuments to the Lost Cause: Women, Art, and the Landscapes of Southern Memory* (Knoxville: University of Tennessee Press, 2003).

3. John Neff, *Honoring the Civil War Dead: Commemoration and the Problem of Reconciliation* (Lawrence: University Press of Kansas, 2005), 148.

4. John Neff gives an excellent overview of federal efforts regarding the burying and reburying of Union dead. See ibid., 103–41. Ladies Memorial Association of Columbus, Georgia, quoted in ibid., 149.

5. Blair, *Cities of the Dead*, 77–105; Georgia newspaper quoted in Neff, *Honoring the Civil War Dead*, 146; *Richmond Whig* quoted in Blair, *Cities of the Dead*, 88.

6. Quoted in Neff, *Honoring the Civil War Dead*, 149.

7. The central symbolic role of white women in Lost Cause work is discussed in W. Scott Poole, *Never Surrender: Confederate Memory and Conservatism in the South Carolina Upcountry* (Athens: University of Georgia Press, 2004), 67–69.

8. Laura Martin Rose, "Address on Dedication of Mississippi Monument to Confederate Women," June 3, 1912, in Brown, *Public Art of Civil War Commemoration*, 77; Blight, *Race and Reunion*, 286–87.

9. *Confederate Veteran* quoted in Blight, *Race and Reunion*, 277.

10. Grace Hale, *Making Whiteness: The Culture of Segregation in the South, 1890–1940* (New York: Random House, 1998), 88–93.

11. Rutherford quoted in ibid., 86.

12. Northern complicity in sentimentalizing the memory of the wartime South, and in feminizing the representation of the Civil War South in the late nineteenth century, is discussed in Nina Silber, *The Romance of Reunion: Northerners and the South, 1865–1900* (Chapel Hill: University of North Carolina Press, 1993). Curator quoted in ibid., 107. On the women's Civil War memorial, see Brown, *Public Art of Civil War Commemoration*, 61.

13. *Ladies Home Journal* story quoted in Silber, *Romance of Reunion*, 118.

14. Thomas J. Brown, "The Confederate Retreat to Mars and Venus," in *Battle Scars: Gender and Sexuality in the American Civil War*, ed. Catherine Clinton and Nina Silber (New York: Oxford University Press, 2006), 189–213.

15. Robert Penn Warren makes the point that "in the moment of its death the Confederacy entered upon its immortality." See Robert Penn Warren, *The Legacy of the Civil War* (1961; reprint, Cambridge, MA: Harvard University Press, 1983), 15; W. Fitzhugh Brundage, *The Southern Past: A Clash of Race and Memory* (Cambridge, MA: Harvard University Press, 2005), 12–54.

16. Elizabeth Stuart Phelps, *The Gates Ajar*, edited by Helen Sootin Smith (Cambridge, MA: Harvard University Press, 1964); Lyde Cullen Sizer, *The Political Work of Northern Women Writers and the Civil War, 1850–1872* (Chapel Hill: University of North Carolina Press, 2000), 264–66.

17. Postwar commemorative volumes included Frank Moore, *Women of the War: Their Heroism and Self-Sacrifice* (Hartford, CT: S. S. Scranton & Co., 1866), and L. P. Brockett and Mary C. Vaughan, *Woman's Work in the Civil War: A Record of Heroism, Patriotism, and Patience* (Philadelphia: Zeigler, Mc-Curdy, 1867), 55. Mary Livermore, *My Story of the War: The Civil War Memoirs of the Famous Nurse, Relief Organizer and Suffragette* (New York: Da Capo Press, 1995), 9. A similar treatment—documenting northern women's heroism during the war to help make the case for political rights in the late nineteenth century—can also be seen in Elizabeth Cady Stanton, Susan B. Anthony, and Matilda Gage, eds., *History of Woman Suffrage*, vol. 2 (New York: Fowler and Wells, 1882), 1–3.

18. Nina Silber, *Daughters of the Union: Northern Women Fight the Civil War* (Cambridge, MA: Harvard University Press, 2005), 268–69.

19. Minutes of the Headquarters Leo W. Myers Relief Corps, WRC chapter of Lincoln, Illinois, June 1, 1888–January 5, 1893, in the Illinois State Historical Library, Springfield, IL; Woman's Relief Corps, *Journal of the Fourteenth National Convention of the Woman's Relief Corps* (Boston, 1896), 207–9.

20. On the WRC recognition of and campaign for Union army nurses see Silber, *Daughters of the Union*, 272, 274.

21. Kathleen Clark, "Making History: African American Commemorative Celebrations in Augusta, Georgia, 1865–1913," in Mills and Simpson, ed., *Monuments to the Lost Cause*, 53–54.

22. Michigan Memorial Day speaker quoted in Amy E. Holmes, "'Such is the Price we Pay': American Widows and the Civil War Pension System," in *Toward a Social History of the Civil War*, ed. Maris Vinovskis (New York: Cambridge University Press, 1990), 194; Stuart McConnell, *Glorious Contentment: The Grand Army of the Republic, 1865–1900* (Chapel Hill: University of North Carolina Press, 1992), 219.

23. Elizabeth Stuart Phelps Ward, "Comrades," in *Civil War Women*, ed. Frank McSherry Jr., Charles G. Waugh, and Martin Greenberg (New York: Simon and Schuster, 1990), 152, 154, 155–56.

24. Woman's Relief Corps, *Journal of the Fifth National Convention of the Woman's Relief Corps, Auxiliary to the Grand Old Army of the Republic* (Boston, 1887), 39; Woman's Relief Corps, Department of Massachusetts, letter of May 5, 1888, in Papers of Massachusetts Woman's Relief Corps, Schlesinger Library, Harvard University, Cambridge, MA; Woman's Relief Corps, *Journal of the Ninth National Convention of the Woman's Relief Corps* (Boston, 1891), 109.

25. Woman's Relief Corps, *Journal of the Eighteenth National Convention of the Woman's Relief Corps* (Boston, 1900), 235; Minutes of the E. A. Brown chapter of the Wisconsin Woman's Relief Corps, for February 22, 1893, Woman's Relief Corps, Department of Wisconsin Records (microfilm), reel 5, Wisconsin Historical Society, Madison; Woman's Relief Corps, *Journal of the Fifteenth National Convention* (Boston, 1897), 148–49.

26. Woman's Relief Corps, *Journal of the Tenth National Convention* (Boston, 1892), 126; Brundage, *The Southern Past*, 60, 83–88.

27. Susie King Taylor, *Reminiscences of My Life in Camp with the 33d United States Colored Troops Late 1st S.C. Volunteers*, electronic ed. (Boston, 1902), 59–60; Frances E. W. Harper, *Iola Leroy; or, Shadows Uplifted* (New York: Oxford University Press, 1988), 130.

28. Woman's Relief Corps, *Journal of the Fifth National Convention of the Woman's Relief Corps* (Boston, 1887), 39; Francesca Morgan, *Women and Patriotism in Jim Crow America* (Chapel Hill: University of North Carolina Press, 2005), 39.

29. Theda Skocpol, *Protecting Soldiers and Mothers: The Political Origins of Social Policy in the United States* (Cambridge, MA: Belknap Press of Harvard University Press, 1992).

Epilogue

1. For more on Scarlett's modernness see Elizabeth Fox-Genovese, "Scarlett O'Hara: The Southern Lady as New Woman," *American Quarterly* 33 (Fall 1981): 391–411; Tony Horwitz, *Confederates in the Attic: Dispatches from the Unfinished Civil War* (New York: Pantheon Books, 1998), 282–311.

Index